Adapting and Extending Secondary Mathematics Activities

New Tasks for Old

OWL

Stephanie Prestage and Pat Perks

David Fulton Publishers
London

David Fulton Publishers Ltd
Ormond House, 26–27 Boswell Street, London WC1N 3JZ

www.fultonpublishers.co.uk

First published in Great Britain by David Fulton Publishers 2001

Note: The rights of Stephanie Prestage and Pat Perks to be identified as the authors of this work has been asserted by them in accordance with the Copyright, Designs and Patents Act 1988.

British Library Cataloguing in Publication Data
A catalogue record for this book is available from the British Library

ISBN 1–85346–712–X

The publishers would like to thank Kate Williams for copy-editing and Sophie Cox for proofreading this book.

Typeset by Elite Typesetting Techniques, Eastleigh, Hampshire
Printed in Great Britain by The Cromwell Press Ltd, Trowbridge, Wilts.

Contents

This is dedicated to the many students, teachers and friends, especially Shirley and Sue, who have worked with us over the years. We have pinched their ideas and used their enthusiasm to maintain our love of mathematics. We acknowledge our debt and offer our heartfelt thanks.

Introduction

We have been thinking about this book for many years. We change tasks easily, but our job is now to help others develop this expertise. Much of the material has been tried out on our Initial Teacher Education (ITE) students following a one-year Postgraduate Certificate in Education (PGCE) for secondary mathematics at the University of Birmingham.

We have always thought of this book as 'new tasks for old' (with the word 'mathematical' being engraved on our hearts). However, unlike Aladdin, who was cheated when his princess fell for the cry 'new lamps for old', we hope you will not feel that our cry is a confidence trick. We have a vision of Aladdin's wonderful lamp being used to transform any mathematical task into one that will challenge pupils at different levels, offer them practice, help their confidence and above all allow you and your pupils to enjoy mathematics.

Stephanie Prestage and Pat Perks
Birmingham
February 2001

CHAPTER 1

Putting mathematics at the heart

Where we introduce why we work in this way

Why this book?

As we work in classrooms or with our students we often design different tasks, or help others to do so. We have much experience of designing tasks and we are often asked where we get our ideas from. Well, like everyone else, we borrow them from others. We then adapt them to the needs of our pupils. Our sources are other teachers, textbooks, journals like *Mathematics in School, Mathematics Teaching* and *Micromaths* and plenty of discussion! Only by talking about mathematics do we refine our ideas. By trying to make our ways of working explicit to our students we have begun to realise that ideas for adapting do not 'just happen' but are based on various strategies. This book explains the techniques we use for creating different tasks for use in the mathematics classroom.

Why do we need different tasks? You will be familiar with the reasons.

- Learners learn in different ways: some need to work from simple to hard cases; some need a challenge before they want to look at simpler ideas; some need more practice than others; some need pictures; and some like the abstract. We cannot cater for this by only working in one way.
- Different environments call for different tasks. For example, you will be aware of the dangers of using scissors with a rowdy Year 7 on a wet Friday afternoon; you cannot move around in a classroom designed for 20 if you have 35 pupils in the group; and just before examinations your focus is bound to be on practice.
- Children work at different rates. The fast ones deserve something more mathematically satisfying than racing ahead in the book or more practice of the same. Children who are mathematically able ought to expand their thinking more widely.

- Some children need more challenging work. Giving a pupil 20 more questions is no reward for getting the first 50 correct.
- Topics need revisiting. We need to find ways of practising familiar ideas in the context of current work.
- 'Variety is the spice of life.'

Textbooks are one of the major resources in mathematics classrooms. They tend, however, to offer one style of working: step-by-step, working from simpler tasks to harder tasks. The books are usually organised to keep much of the content separate, with the idea that this will make the learning and the accounting for delivering the curriculum easier. Most questions, or parts of questions, have only one answer. Contexts are provided, and the formats of the questions often seem very different as you work through an exercise. However, the questions have been well thought through. The ideas are based on the type of work on which your pupils will be assessed. There will be many diagrams and contexts, pictures and facts that you can use to interest your pupils. Textbooks contain lots of practice in a particular style. All of this is very useful, but if we believe that learners need different experiences, textbooks need to be supplemented.

Some pupils find the examples in textbooks far too easy and become bored. Extending activities to include generalisation and proof may provide just the challenge needed to keep their enthusiasm for mathematics. Some pupils do not understand the questions in the book. If they work on the mathematics using an adapted task they can often approach the questions on a later occasion with a greater confidence and competence. For example, the fishing competition task in Chapter 3 was devised as a result of pupils having difficulty understanding the questions on decimals in their textbook; they knew neither what to do nor how to do it. The time spent playing the game in a lesson resulted in most of the children tackling a homework sheet with success and remembering their work on decimals with enthusiasm.

By creating different tasks we can begin to work on the ideas outlined earlier. We design tasks which match our beliefs about what should go on in mathematics classrooms.

- We want the mathematics in any task to be explicit. Our pupils are learning mathematics; they need to know what it is.
- Separating different aspects of the curriculum can cause confusion for some pupils. Pupils can often confuse perimeter and area of rectangles unless we work, at some point, on these two attributes together and look at the relationship between them or lack of one. Is it true that area and perimeter are connected for regular polygons? How able a mathematician do you need to be to work on such questions?
- By connecting the curriculum, the number of topics we have to teach becomes less daunting.

- If we practise some content in the context of other content, we are keeping the ideas fresh in pupils' minds and giving ourselves more time.
- Practice needs to be purposeful. There needs to be a reason for doing the mathematics that is not just about getting the right answer.
- When each question has only one right answer, the emotional investment in that answer is huge. If questions have more than one answer the emotional commitment lessens, but the opportunity for helping pupils increases, without killing the question. How many times have you found yourself solving a problem for a pupil? It is fascinating to watch how pupils manipulate our students into doing their work for them.
- One of our responsibilities is to ensure that our pupils get the best examination results they can. We believe that the best way to do this is to challenge pupils to answer questions which go wider than the ones they will meet in such examinations.
- To get better (and more) mathematicians, we do not need to race through the curriculum, but should offer our pupils challenging tasks based on the content everyone is doing.
- The first attainment target (Ma1), 'Using and Applying Mathematics', should be integrated into the mathematics curriculum as much as possible. It is not an add on: it describes a way of working mathematically.

The new National Curriculum (Department for Education and Employment (DfEE) 1999) has been written so that the integration of Ma1 with the other attainment targets is explicit in the programmes of study. One of the ways of increasing coverage of Ma1 in lessons is to expect pupils to make choices, so that decision-making becomes one of the skills worked on in mathematics lessons. This also links with purpose. If a pupil is asked to find the value of $2a + b$ when $a = 3$ and $b = -1$, the pupil has no choices to make. If the question is given a purpose, and becomes 'When is $2a + b$ smaller than $a - b$?', the practice of substitution is subsumed into the finding of the relationship; pupils have to choose the numbers to substitute and there is plenty of practice because there are many answers. There is also differentiation because some pupils will solve an equation and offer a justification for the results (probably because they do not need to practice substitution).

The desire to offer all pupils a rich mathematical experience and to enhance their learning and enjoyment of the subject is at the heart of the way in which we work. If we offer appropriate challenges the brightest can be encouraged to develop their mathematics more widely and we can help the low achiever to learn better – and we can enjoy mathematics. As teachers we need to use all the sources available to us to help improve our pupils' learning.

The purpose of this book

This book is intended to accompany all your current sources, your scheme and your textbooks and worksheets. The techniques are intended to offer you another way of looking at any of these materials to create more diversity of tasks. The other major resource in schools, other than textbooks and worksheets, is the computer. Technology has become a major player in the field of mathematics. We need to question its role and the implications of the subject and not forget the humbler incarnations of Information and Communications Technology (ICT): calculators. Using existing ideas and adapting them to suit particular needs can provide a multitude of new problems. Adapting your own tasks creates a versatility in the teacher which can make you more responsive to the needs of the classroom.

In Chapter 2 we introduce you to ways we begin to think more carefully about the mathematics in tasks, and Chapter 3 offers initial examples of taking tasks and adapting them in ways that are explored in more detail in later chapters. The first structured technique we offer is in Chapter 4. We change tasks by adding or removing parts of the task, changing the givens or constraints. Changing resources can be a major way of adapting tasks, whether the resources are varied (Chapter 6) or focus around technology (Chapter 7), or depending on what the learner brings to the task (Chapters 8 and 9). Chapter 10 looks more explicitly at linking the syllabus together and Chapter 11 uses these ideas together with the length of time given to a task to define the many aspects the teacher has to choose when planning for pupils' learning.

We hope you find the techniques useful. Remember, we want our pupils to learn mathematics, so put mathematics at the heart of any task.

CHAPTER 2

A splurge of ideas

In which we offer ways to connect subject knowledge across the mathematics curriculum and meet existing techniques for opening up questions

This chapter is in two sections. The first section looks at two existing approaches which we have found useful for changing and adapting questions. We thought that you should know where our ideas are rooted. The second section considers a technique that we use throughout the book to capture ideas at any particular time. We will create diagrams that we call 'splurge' diagrams (hence 'a splurge of ideas'), although elsewhere in the literature they are referred to as brainstorming, topic webs or concept maps. When analysing the mathematics within a particular topic, much of our knowledge comes from years of experience with different texts, questions and discussions. Trying to access this knowledge can be rather hit and miss, so a splurge of ideas related to the topic can be useful: we use whatever emerges on the day. The lack of linearity is crucial (there is no right route) and encourages the jotting down of any ideas which might indicate the breadth of choices within a topic. Later in this chapter we will 'splurge' ideas about resources, mathematical content and mathematical processes. Every time we draw such a diagram it may have different connections and different words, often with new links in whatever area of the curriculum we are working in. We are sure many of the ideas will be familiar to you, but we hope you enjoy our interpretation.

Technique 1: 'What-if-not'

One of the most interesting techniques for analysing alternative approaches to finding new questions, as well as analysing the mathematics, is that described by Stephen Brown and Marion Walter in their articles in *Mathematics Teaching* and their book *The Art of Problem Posing* (Brown and Walter 1990). With apologies to them we will attempt to give you a brief flavour of the technique, but we recommend that you go and read the book itself.

Take a familiar question:

> Complete the sequence 4, 9, 14, 19, 24, _, _.

Most of us know how to respond. The answer is 29 and 34. The question is routine, but we are about to play with this question to give some alternatives.

The first thing that Brown and Walter suggest is that you list all the attributes of the question (we sometimes use the word 'givens'):

- the first five numbers in the sequence are given;
- we need to find two more;
- we need to find the sixth and the seventh numbers;
- the first number is 4;
- the second is 9;
- the first two numbers are square;
- the fourth number is prime;
- the pattern in the units digits goes 4, 9, 4, 9, …;
- the numbers are even, odd, even, odd, even, …;
- each number is a multiple of 5, subtract 1;
- each number is a multiple of 5, add 4;
- and so on.

Who would have thought there was so much to say? The first time we tried this our list was much shorter, but like many things finding the attributes in a question gets easier with practice.

Secondly (say Brown and Walter), take one of the attributes from the list and ask the question 'What if it is not … [the attribute], but … [something else]?'

> What if the first five numbers are not given, and only the first two are? The question becomes:
> Complete the sequence 4, 9, _, _, _,…

A lot more mathematics and practice about sequences is needed to answer this question since there are many solutions. And since there are many solutions the pupils will have to record (and perhaps even justify) the answers.

Here are some more changes.

> What if only one term is given and it is the fifth? Find five sequences which have 24 as the fifth term.

There are infinite solutions here, so we have included a constraint ('Find five …'). You may want to introduce a similar constraint to the following task.

What if the first two numbers are square, but the second number is not 9. The task offered might be:
- Complete the sequence 4, 16, 28, 40, 52, _, _.
- Complete the sequence 4, 16, 64, 256, _, _.

What if the sequence is not a multiple of 5, subtract 1, but subtract 2, or subtract 3, or subtract 4 or subtract 5 …? Complete these sequences and find a common link:
- 3, 8, 13, 18, _, _
- 2, 7, 12, 17, _, _
- 1, 6, 11, _, _.

So, by changing some of the givens in the question, we have generated new possibilities for the classroom. Although the technique has not offered big changes to the original question on sequences, it has created the chance to work on some bigger ideas in mathematics. The focus for the solver in the final alternative above is not just on two correct responses, but how this number sequence relates to many others. However, there is a word of warning! Having found some new questions you do then need to analyse the results to see if you have generated something worthwhile! This will become apparent in later chapters (in particular see Chapter 5) as we become mildly outrageous in our suggestions for changes to questions.

It is possible to use the 'What-if-not' technique on all types of questions. A favourite task we have used with students aged from 6 upwards is the problem of the elephant and the buns (Figure 2.1) (Perks and Prestage 1992); where it comes from we do not know. (This form of the problem works well with the under 12s and the over 16s, but for other teenagers the bun house becomes the hold of a boat which has sunk in shark-infested waters, with gold bars instead of buns and a treasure-seeking diver instead of an elephant.)

If you have not come across this problem before, you may like to do the mathematics before reading on. Now list the attributes of the problem. Some of our ideas about a few attributes are given in Table 2.1.

The attributes now offer ways of altering the question to explore new questions, and ways of developing the question into generalisations, and because the original question was challenging, so are the adaptations. It is useful to work on this technique as we have found that it develops a flexibility of thinking about questions and about mathematics which is useful in adapting and finding new questions. The technique is also useful for pupils. The processes in Ma1 expect pupils to make and monitor choices; 'What-if-not' offers a way of approaching this.

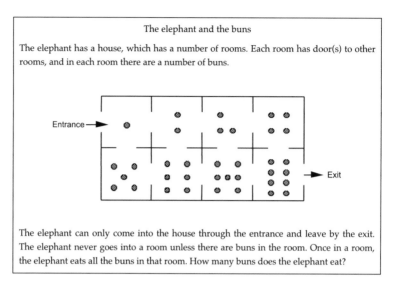

The elephant and the buns

The elephant has a house, which has a number of rooms. Each room has door(s) to other rooms, and in each room there are a number of buns.

The elephant can only come into the house through the entrance and leave by the exit. The elephant never goes into a room unless there are buns in the room. Once in a room, the elephant eats all the buns in that room. How many buns does the elephant eat?

Figure 2.1 The elephant and the buns

Table 2.1 Attributes of the elephant and buns problem

Attribute	What-if-not!
There are eight rooms	What if there are not eight rooms but ten, twelve, six, nine …?
The rooms are square	What if the rooms are not square but triangular?
The doors are all open	What if the doors are not all open, but some of them are shut?
The number of buns goes 1, 2, 3, 4, 5, 6, 7, 8	What if the number of buns goes 4, 5, 6, 7, …, 11 or 3, 6, 9, 12, …, or 101, 102, 103, …?

Technique 2: PCAI

One area which suffers from the 'do the mathematics because it is there' syndrome, is data handling. We have watched pupils as they are taught how to tally 'because they have to learn how to tally' rather than because it might be useful in keeping track of data in some circumstances. There is little purpose to the activities we see in some of our students' lessons on data handling other than learning skills such as drawing bar charts, calculating the mean and so on. There seems to be little point in pupils doing the work they are given, especially in this technological age when computers will draw pie charts, bar charts, calculate the mean, etc.

PCAI is an acronym for the data handling cycle illustrated in Figure 2.2. (These strands are also used in Ma4, 'Handling data', in the National Curriculum.)

Stage 1   P – pose the question
Stage 2   C – collect the data (collecting and recording)

Stage 3   A – analyse the data (processing and representing)
Stage 4   I – interpret the results (interpreting) (Graham 1991: 97).

In describing an approach to statistics, the PCAI cycle also offers some insight into how we have learned how to adapt tasks. For any activity (P) we collect the mathematical data (C) and analyse it (A). In the interpretation stage (I) our question becomes 'What mathematics do we want pupils to do?' This in turn leads to new questions (back to P). This is a simplification, but these four stages are part of the cycles we go through.

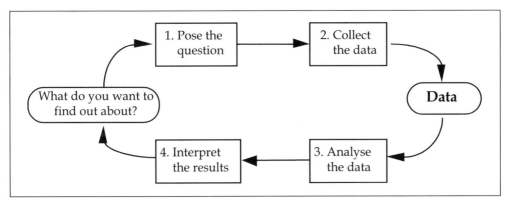

Figure 2.2 The PCAI cycle (adapted from Graham 1991)

In his article 'Where is the "P" in statistics' (Graham 1991), Alan Graham looks at the PCAI cycle in order to explore the reason for using statistics. Children often collect data, and they analyse it. Sometimes they interpret it. Do you remember those examination questions where you were given data, had to draw a bar chart, and finally were asked 'Comment on the data'? We certainly remember the trite responses. How can one interpret data unless you know what purpose the interpretation was for. We can all remember campaigns where the same data were used to 'prove' two opposite sides of an argument. Whilst we realise that interpretation does not need to be partisan, it makes more sense if you know why you have collected the data. If you consider what question you wish to ask, the rest of the process has some purpose; the interpretation becomes slanted towards answering the question, or it may enable you to raise new questions.

A question often used to collect data in the secondary classroom in order to practise drawing a statistical diagram is 'In which month were you born?' It is easy enough to collect the data; you could ask for a show of hands. It is straightforward to draw the diagram. But then what? Why do we want to know? There would be more to consider if the question were something such as 'I have just been told that more babies are born in the winter than in the summer. Do you think that is true?' We would then have to decide what data to collect (much the same as before), and what we mean by 'winter' and 'summer', and these could then be used to interpret a diagram for the results in our class. The question could then be explored by gathering more data. 'If it is true for our class, is it true for the rest of the school?' 'If it is true for our school, how reliable are our conclusions?' The question now begins to offer a purpose for the data handling.

A wider implication for all teachers in their planning is to find a clear purpose in the activities pupils are asked to do (other than getting it right and getting the ticks). In Chapter 1 we talked about our belief in purposeful practice. In statistics there needs to be a purpose in collecting the data in order to have analysis and interpretation which has some meaning. But the PCAI cycle also reminds us that other areas of mathematics need a purpose for practice. This may be as simple as practising times tables while playing multiplication Bingo, the purpose being to win; or finding how to deduce the number of factors any number has, which offers excellent practice for finding factors and expressing numbers as products of primes. From PCAI, then, we take away the reminders of analysing and interpreting, and, crucially, the place of purpose.

Splurge diagrams

There have been many other influences on our thinking over the years as well as these two techniques as we try to make how we work more explicit: work on investigations; different textbooks (we both taught with the original SMP, so we met 'modern maths' as teachers); and, most importantly, work with our students. One tool we use all the time is the splurge diagram. Drawing splurge diagrams can be difficult to start with, but they do become more and more useful as you create more of them.

Splurge diagrams for mathematics

How well connected is your subject knowledge across the mathematics curriculum? Hearing the words 'bar charts' or 'solving equations', what mathematics is conjured up in your mind? Put the words 'bar chart' in the middle of a page and write down all the things you can think of that come to mind when you teach about bar charts. What kinds of mathematics, skills, techniques and resources do you use? What do you want your pupils to come to know about bar charts? How will you use these ideas when you are working on other aspects of the mathematics curriculum? What do the pupils need to be able to do, now and in the future? Put down all your ideas. This is what we call a splurge diagram, with all your ideas splurged around the original word, interconnected with lines. The more words you can write down, the better you will be aware of the connections in your subject knowledge. We try and fill an A4 page.

The following examples of splurge diagrams about bar charts and solving equations (Figures 2.3 and 2.4) are not meant to be exhaustive; they reflect our thinking about these topics at the time of writing this book. Your own splurge diagram will probably make much more sense to you than ours will because the range of ideas and the order we present them in may be too large to take in at once. In fact, it is better to draw these diagrams with another colleague so that you can share ideas.

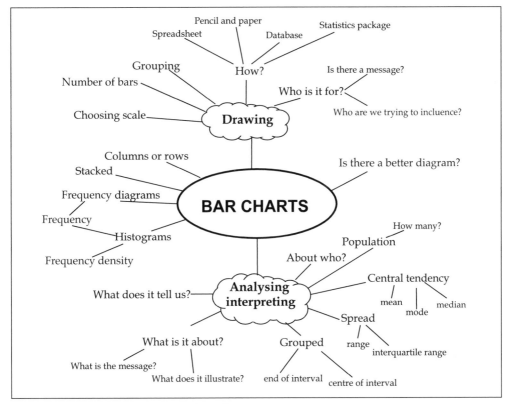

Figure 2.3 Splurge diagram for bar charts

Bar charts are generally drawn to represent some data and to help with interpretation of that data (remember PCAI), which is why the diagram has two main subsections. As well as the mathematics there are also the 'purpose' prompts, and with the ready use of ICT there is a wealth of different types of charts that might be drawn, so we need to question whether the bar chart is the best diagram. All of these things are represented on our diagram. When it comes to planning for teaching, questions about bar charts may reflect many of the aspects given in the diagram or just one. Hopefully, over the many occasions that pupils meet bar charts, most of these aspects will be considered so that a pupil who knows about bar charts will be able to deal with these many different areas.

Figure 2.4 is a splurge diagram for solving equations. Some of the content is given, but you may like to add 'methods of solution' and 'resources' to it.

The splurge diagrams that we have created for these two areas of mathematics are very different. Figure 2.3 uses more questions and is grouped more strongly than Figure 2.4. Figure 2.3 also seems to range over the statistics syllabus more thoroughly than the algebraic connections offered in Figure 2.4. Such differences do not matter. You will draw something very different from these, as will we the next time we draw them, but each time you draw them you begin to realise how the curriculum can become more and more connected.

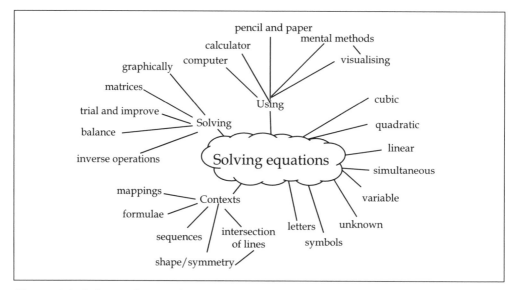

Figure 2.4 Splurge diagram for solving equations

Mathematical content words need not be the only source for splurge diagrams. Process words from Ma1 might also be used. Figure 2.5 shows a splurge diagram for 'explaining', which is explicitly part of Ma1, as well as being a skill that it is worth our pupils developing.

The explaining diagram took us to justifying and then to proof. What if we were to begin with proof? Proof could be the starting point for your thinking, but again you would need to consider this within the framework of the mathematical topics for the pupils you are teaching. This might lead to a diagram such as that shown in Figure 2.6.

The diagram in Figure 2.6 is mixed. Some words are there to help to remember the stages towards proving; some words reflect content; others describe the beginnings of tasks. The style of the splurge does not matter as long as you begin to record the connections and try to see ways of integrating your ideas. You may come up with something you had not considered before as the recording offers you the context to challenge yourself. The opportunities for developing these ideas in the classroom become more obvious the more you work with such diagrams. Putting down on paper possible routes, connections and relationships makes clearer the prior knowledge needed by the pupils, and possible knowledge they may acquire. You become aware of the infinite variety and the choices you might make.

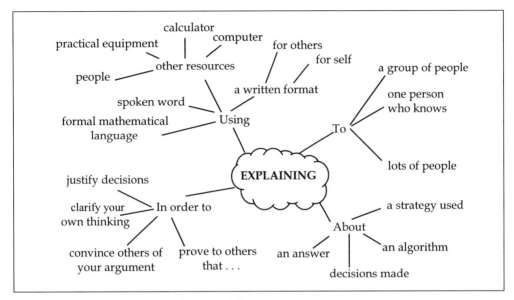

Figure 2.5 Splurge diagram for explaining

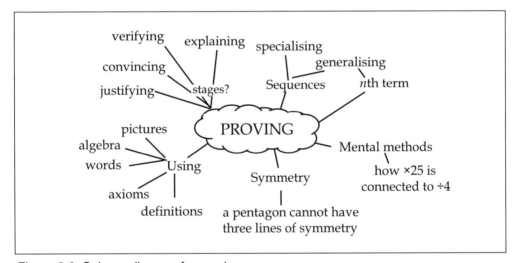

Figure 2.6 Splurge diagram for proving

Splurge diagrams for teaching

Constructing splurge diagrams is not limited to finding out about mathematics but can be adapted to help consider the variety of resources, mathematical skills or other aspects that impact on a lesson (e.g. Perks and Prestage 1994). The style of lesson comes from the choice of activities used, which in turn is based on decisions about the ways in which pupils will be working, what resources will be used, the length of the activity and the outcomes the teacher hopes to see. Any of these aspects to planning lessons could be placed at the centre of a splurge diagram.

Resources

The splurge diagram in Figure 2.7 offers an extra section for 'solving equations' and splurges ideas about the use of resources in more detail. (We will return to this idea in Chapter 6.) There are huge implications for the mathematics here (something that we will pick up again in Chapter 5). For example, if a pupil is required to solve $2x + 7 = 19$ using a graphical calculator that expects you to input in the form '$y =$', they first have to consider using the equation $y = 2x + 7$ and then possibly look for coordinates of the intersection of this line with $y = 19$. If a pupil is required to solve $2x + 7 = 19$ using a trial and improvement method then the prior knowledge requirements are very different.

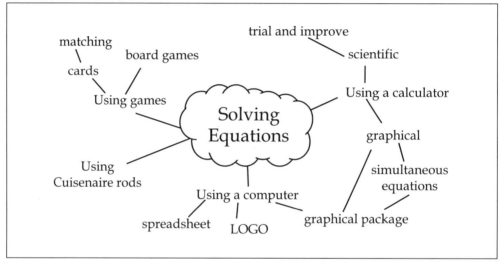

Figure 2.7 Splurge diagram for resources for solving equations

Occasionally we challenge ourselves to add things to a splurge diagram that are not normally associated with a topic to see if we can create a new activity and rethink the connections in the mathematics. For example, we have added LOGO to the possible resources in Figure 2.7, although it is not usually associated with solving equations. This then challenges us to come up with an idea: well, equations are about variables and LOGO uses variables. You could write a procedure with the variable d to get the two turtles starting from the same point to draw two lines, lines such as $d + 100$ and $2*d + 20$. Figure 2.8 shows a procedure and the results when $d = 20$. The challenge then is to make the two lines the same length by altering the value of d: that is, the pupils would be working on finding a solution to $d + 100 = 2d + 20$. There are three arrows as the original turtle is 0. You know you have solved the problem when you can only see two arrows.

Different resources lead to different ways of approaching the solving of equations. The images we offer to pupils will be different as a result.

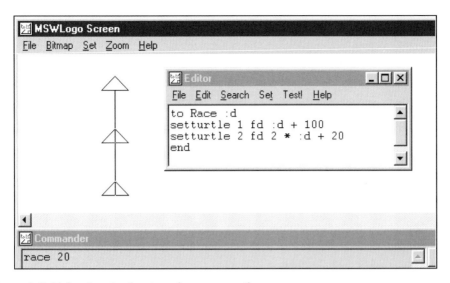

Figure 2.8 Using two turtles to solve an equation

Another way of approaching resources is to consider a particular task: for example, constructing an equilateral triangle using different techniques or instruments (see Figure 2.9). The starting point may be what you can remember of how to do the construction. You may remember learning, for example, to use a ruler and protractor to construct an equilateral triangle. Then you ask (in the spirit of this book) 'what-if-not' a protractor, and see what you can replace it with. If you know how to create a square from folding a rectangle of paper, you may be curious

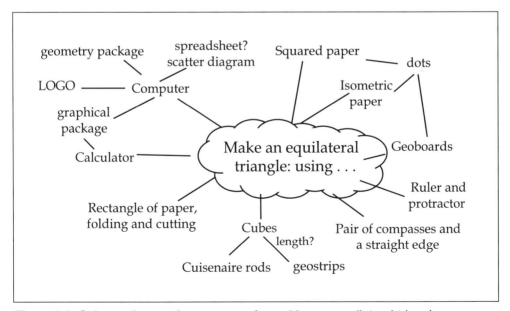

Figure 2.9 Splurge diagram for resources for making an equilateral triangle

to see if this technique can be used for an equilateral triangle. The computer offers another way of making equilateral triangles. There are the more obvious choices in software – geometry packages or LOGO – but we could ask about other software to see if this extends our thinking. Try to think of any resource. You may or may not be able to use it but at least it will remind you of possibilities. (Chapter 6 explores these ideas further, in particular detailing the consequences of changes resources on the mathematics that might be practised by the pupils.)

Discussion
'Discussion' is often mentioned in our students' lesson plans. Talk is an important aspect of teaching and learning and we return to it in Chapter 8. Using a lesson where discussion is the major focus leads us to think of mathematical topics and types of activity or contexts which would promote discussion, such as:
- working in pairs or groups;
- reporting to others and deciding key points;
- sharing ideas, perceptions, images;
- resolving conflict, between people and information;
- needing to make decisions, with multiple answers or reasons;
- justifying decisions;
- using materials such as cards or diagrams to sort or justify decisions;
- using computers.

This list has been included in the next splurge diagram (Figure 2.10). Also in this diagram is a selection of possible topics for discussion.

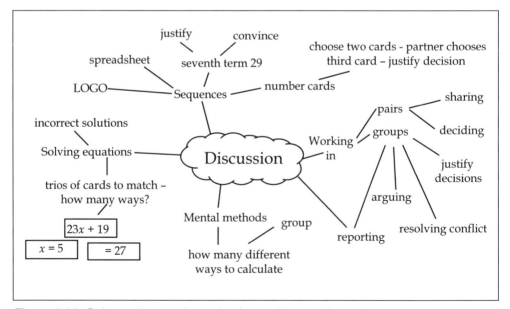

Figure 2.10 Splurge diagram for topics for working on discussion

Some tasks have already been added to the diagram; the use of cards to provoke discussion suggested some activities and the justifying and convincing branches suggested others. Then you will have to decide on the management of the task and how all the different aspects will influence the lesson style.

Being mathematical

Each of these tools offers a way in which we approach mathematics and its teaching. For us the purpose of teaching is to encourage children to be mathematical. By analysing the mathematics across a topic as in Figures 2.3 and 2.4 we are making ourselves more aware of the connections within the subject and the possible contexts for working on the mathematics. 'What-if-not' allows us to examine questions in detail and to extend their mathematical content. PCAI reminds us to offer purpose to our activities; if we want pupils to justify or interpret there must be something for them to justify or interpret.

Splurge diagrams offer a structure for considering the other elements of our teaching which will affect our design of tasks. By recording connections we can begin to consider ways to make these connections explicit to our pupils, thus helping their learning. By integrating ideas we can find that the teaching syllabus can be more manageable.

References

Brown, S. I. and Walter, M. I. (1990) *The Art of Problem Posing*, 2nd edn. London: Lawrence Erlbaum Associates.

Department for Education and Employment (DfEE) (1999) *Mathematics: The National Curriculum for England*. London: The Stationery Office.

Graham, A. (1991) 'Where is the "P" in statistics?', in Pimm, D. and Love, E. (eds) *Teaching and Learning School Mathematics*. London: Hodder & Stoughton.

Perks, P. and Prestage, S. (1992) 'Making choices (3): choices, constraints and control', *Mathematics in Schools* 21(5), 44–5.

Perks, P. and Prestage, S. (1994) 'Planning for learning', in Jaworski, B. and Watson, A. (eds) *Mentoring in Mathematics Teaching*. London: Falmer.

CHAPTER 3

New questions for old

In which we discover how to change questions just a little bit and analyse the consequences

Take an old question, change it a bit and, hey presto, a new question appears. What do these changes look like? What kind of changes could you make? Well, that is what this chapter is about. We will give you a flavour of the type of alterations that you might make and how it affects the mathematics for the pupils. We will return to some of these questions later in the book in order to analyse them in further detail. We encourage you to be as imaginative as possible knowing that you can always ditch your wildest imaginings. Sometimes the results are good and sometimes they are not so good. You need to be able to tell the difference and eventually determine your own criteria for what is 'good'. An important criterion for us is that a new idea will provide a starting point accessible to all those students to whom it is offered and that it offers an opportunity to practise some skills as well as provide some challenge.

Not all of the changes you make to questions will fulfil these requirements but the 'best' will. In the changes that we make, the pupils will often be asked to make some decisions in order to begin to answer the new question, and this is all tied in with integrating aspects of Ma1 in the National Curriculum (see Chapter 1). We also have some of our own rules when changing questions, such as 'it must not take ages to produce' and 'it must not cost much'. You will discover your own priorities.

The technique that we offer in this overview is to consider a task or a textbook question and make a small change to it. What kind of small change? Clearly, there are many ways of altering questions in order to create new tasks, but we have found the following four to be useful.

- Change a bit of an existing question.
- Give the answer, rather than the question.

- Change the resources (with ICT and without ICT).
- Change the format.

We will consider each of these methods in several ways and look at the consequences for the mathematics. The starting points are not original and are adapted from familiar styles of questions. (Hopefully all the starting suggestions will be very familiar!)

Change a bit of the question

The first suggestion that we offer is to take a standard question from a text and alter a small aspect. Different emphases in the mathematics often appear as a result. The following anecdote comes from a secondary teacher.

> Working with a Year 7 class on the angles in a triangle, one of my favourite tasks was to ask them to draw as many triangles as they could with angles of the size 30, 60 and 90 degrees. This would keep them happy for some time. Those who were proficient with their protractors drew several triangles, while I could work with a small group of pupils on their struggles to draw a triangle and use a protractor efficiently. Eventually a rumour would spread around the class that these triangles were all the same. It took some time to decide what was the same, but we had a lot of good discussion as we came to an agreement.
>
> The next question involved a small change. I asked them to draw triangles with angles of size 30, 60 and 80 degrees. They set to with a will: they already knew that there was only one they really needed to draw. The noise level increased. Frustration set in. Eventually someone said, 'It's not fair!' 'Why?' was my response. The consensus was that it could not be done and I was not allowed to set questions that could not be done. When I asked them why it could not be done some of them dug into their memories and said that they had been told at primary school that the angles of a triangle add up to 180 degrees and these angles only added up to 170 degrees. Very few of these pupils ever forgot this fact.

To give an idea of some of the many small changes that might be made, here are a few questions with the alterations beside them, using the topics of subtraction, speed, perimeter, algebraic substitution and formulas. The health warning that comes with these questions and with the whole book is that neither the question nor its alternative is better than the other. Each serves a different purpose for the teacher and for the learner. Crucially, the teacher needs to know for what mathematical purpose any question is being given.

Remove some of the information from the question

A standard calculation can be transformed into one which has a range of solutions by the addition of an ink blot! In the example in Figure 3.1 the hundreds digit has been hidden by the blot.

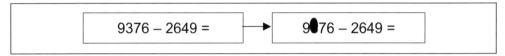

Figure 3.1 Changing a subtraction question

Instead of one sum the pupils now have a possible ten. The calculations are limited to a smallish number but the extra mathematics lies in recognising that the choice of number affects how you solve the problem. You might also ask the pupils questions about place value in the many solutions as the digits alter, in order to generalise about the outcomes (in grown-up terms if the blob is n can you predict the solution – a question for your gifted pupils). You could remove any of the digits, or you might remove two of them.

Part of the question in Figure 3.2 has also been removed.

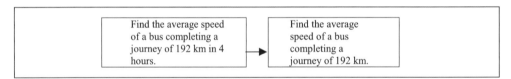

Figure 3.2 Changing a question about average speed

The changed question requires decisions about times: what time is reasonable; what a journey might involve. The pupils could choose the speed and find the time or vice versa. They might include some stopping period. Again there is more practice in the right-hand question and more need for the pupil to record the solution offered.

The diagram on the left of Figure 3.3 shows a typical perimeter problem. The pupil needs to work out the lengths of the unlabelled sides and to calculate the perimeter. The change we have made, similar to the last example, is to remove one of the given lengths.

A consequence of removing one of the lengths is that the question no longer has a single solution, but has many, as happened in the previous examples (you will pick this up as a recurring theme in this book). The pupil has to decide on a missing length and calculate the perimeter. However, the pupil can be encouraged to make different decisions about the missing length and to collect a number of special cases. At one level the perimeter calculation can be made many times (the provision of practice). At another level, it is possible to challenge the pupil to move

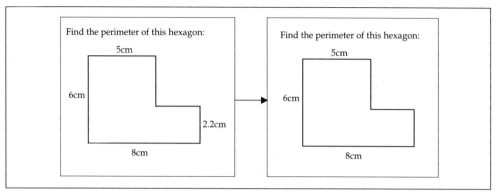

Figure 3.3 Changing a question about the perimeter of a hexagon

from the special cases to the generalisation that the perimeter is always the same! The pupils could then be encouraged to offer a justification for this result. The practice of finding the perimeter of compound shapes is still as strong, but the focus is no longer on the special case, but the general result and the implications for this to the pupils' understanding of perimeter. The task allows for differentiation, offering practice for those that need it yet having sufficient breadth for your mathematically able pupils.

Replace part of the question

In this next set of questions we look at some of the attributes of the questions and replace part of them (see Chapter 2). Figure 3.4 involves algebraic substitution in an angle context and we have used the method of 'what-if-not' to make a change. This question on the left of Figure 3.4 was found in a textbook.

There is only one possible solution to the textbook question. For many pupils this is a difficult question and they only have one chance of getting it correct. The question asks for substitutions into an algebraic formula, perhaps the use of simultaneous equations and for knowledge that the angle sum of a triangle is 180 degrees. If a pupil cannot do the question the teacher has to explain how to begin the solution, perhaps by almost doing the question for the pupil. Then the next

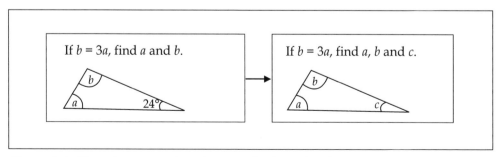

Figure 3.4 Changing a question about angles in a triangle

question in the exercise appears, different from the previous one, and the explanation has to begin all over again.

The changed question, given successfully by one of our ITE students to a bottom set Year 9 group, allows more practice of substitution within the same question. The given angle is 24° and then we ask 'what-if-it-is-not 24°' but c. The teacher can explain 'what to do' while still leaving freedom for the pupil to practise substitution: 'If $b = 60°$, what is the value of a, and the value of c?'. A pupil can be shown once, twice or even more times how to do the question, but there is still plenty of opportunity for a pupil to do their own work on the question. The repetition also allows new questions to emerge from the teacher or the pupils:

- What are the largest possible values of a, b, c?
- Can the triangle be isosceles?
- Can the triangle be right-angled?
- If $c = 24°$, what are the values of a and b (or any other value of c)?

If pupils are asked to draw the triangles a context for the algebra is reinforced, and the value of the angles becomes important (it also provides a check for the arithmetic).

For the formula question in Figure 3.5, the change comes from removing the direct substitution questions and offering some purpose for doing the calculation. The question on the left is fairly straightforward, requiring substitution of three given values, and the solver has no decisions to make. The context could easily be ignored. By adding a question rather than offering a given set of values, the solver has to decide which values to substitute and whether or not there is more than one solution to the problem. There is a purpose for finding the solution; finding the relative ages of the two people named. Justifying the number of possible answers could require the use of a graph or some other algebraic ideas.

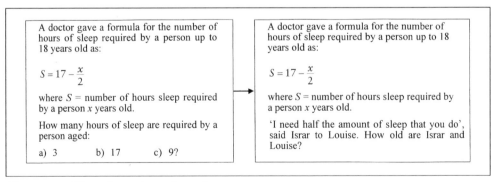

Figure 3.5 Changing a formula task

Add a bit to the question

Figure 3.6 gives a coordinate question which practises plotting coordinates. The idea of finding an isosceles triangle is only incidental, so that you join the points up. By adding a few more coordinates you make the idea of finding isosceles triangles an intrinsic piece of mathematics, as you can see in Figure 3.7.

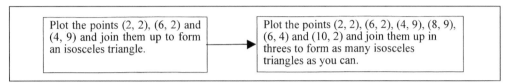

Plot the points (2, 2), (6, 2) and (4, 9) and join them up to form an isosceles triangle.

→ Plot the points (2, 2), (6, 2), (4, 9), (8, 9), (6, 4) and (10, 2) and join them up in threes to form as many isosceles triangles as you can.

Figure 3.6 Adding to a coordinate question

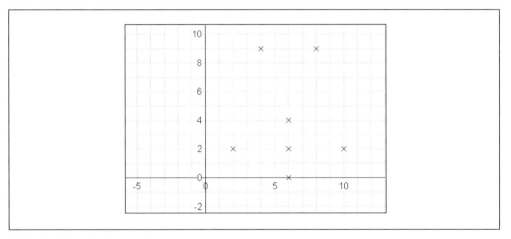

Figure 3.7 Plotting the points in the coordinate question

The question on the left of Figure 3.8 offers only one question. The same context can be added to with extra questions. The pupils could be encouraged to try this with different starting numbers ('What-if-not' 12 and 3 but 15 and 3, or 8 and 2 and so on).

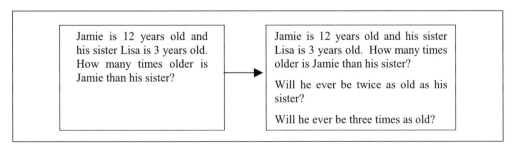

Jamie is 12 years old and his sister Lisa is 3 years old. How many times older is Jamie than his sister?

→ Jamie is 12 years old and his sister Lisa is 3 years old. How many times older is Jamie than his sister?

Will he ever be twice as old as his sister?

Will he ever be three times as old?

Figure 3.8 Adding to an age question

Give the answer

The second way of creating new tasks is to give the answer rather than the question. Textbooks have lots of questions, usually with one answer each. If you look at the information normally found on the answers page you will find a very rich seam of possible tasks, all of which have more than one response.

Typical arithmetic questions might be lots of questions of the form '7 + 8 = _': one question and one solution. Suppose you want to generate a lot of arithmetic practice. Give the answer and not the question.

> The answer is 15. What was the question?

There are clearly hundreds of possible responses to these tasks and this may prevent any work being done at all! If you know what aspect of mathematics you want the pupils to work on then you may wish to limit the choices available by presenting the question focused on a particular area of mathematics. For example, you might give the pupils the question in the following forms (Figure 3.9) in order to practise addition as well as working on number bonds and ideas about infinite solutions. The format of Figure 3.9a only allows the sum of two numbers.

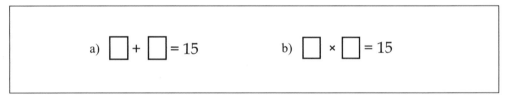

a) $\square + \square = 15$ b) $\square \times \square = 15$

Figure 3.9 Calculations with the answer 15

You might change the operation to persuade pupils to move to multiplication, giving the format for the product of two numbers as in Figure 3.9b. Or you could have three boxes, or four, and so on.

You can leave the pupils working on the question until they demonstrate the level of their knowledge in the area concerned. It is in this situation that you can begin to assess where pupils are confident in their mathematical knowledge.

You may want to change the number set that the pupils are working with, so you might change the 15 to 6.37, −4 or $\frac{5}{7}$. One advantage of offering numbers in different forms is that it may allow you to focus on particular types of numbers or calculations more quickly. An answer like 6.37 may generate a response using decimals more quickly than responses to questions with the answer 15.

There are many areas of mathematics that might be explored in this way in the secondary classroom. Once you begin to consider answers many suggestions appear. So, instead of 'find the area or perimeter of a given rectangle', give the answer.

> **Area of rectangles**
> The area of the rectangle is 12cm². What are the possible lengths and widths of the rectangle?

This is a lovely question for exploring pupils' understanding of the relationship between area and perimeter, factors of 12, or an infinite set of solutions.

The following task is one of our favourite questions for practising applying Pythagoras's theorem. Solving the problem requires the algorithm to be used many times as the pupil makes decisions about the number and types of solutions. This is better than a worksheet any day, and requires little preparation!

> **Pythagoras's theorem**
> What right-angled triangles can you find with an hypotenuse of 17cm?

The next questions have even more possibilities.

> **Equations**
> The solution to a question is $x = 5$. What was the question?
> The solution to an equation is $x = 5$ or $x = -2$. What was the equation?

There are many different equations you could consider, but there are also many different contexts for x as the unknown, especially in the first situation. Perhaps by exploring these different contexts many other aspects of mathematics can become more clear. Figure 3.10 shows our splurge diagram for ideas based around the answer $x = 5$. In your teaching you will choose to constrain the pupils to work on a particular area of mathematics.

This final question in this section gives another situation where working on the special cases may eventually lead to a generalisation about similar triangles. In fact, giving answers in this way often provides lots of practice, as well as a reason for the practice, and may eventually lead to generalisations about the mathematics.

> **Trigonometry**
> The tangent of an angle is $\frac{5}{12}$. What was the question?

Changing the resources

Changing the resources available for solving a problem can often have quite dramatic consequences on the mathematics required for finding a solution. What is required, sometimes, is that resources are limited rather than letting the pupil have a free range from which to choose. The first set of questions shows this quite powerfully. You might pause for a moment to consider the effects of changing the resources upon the mathematics.

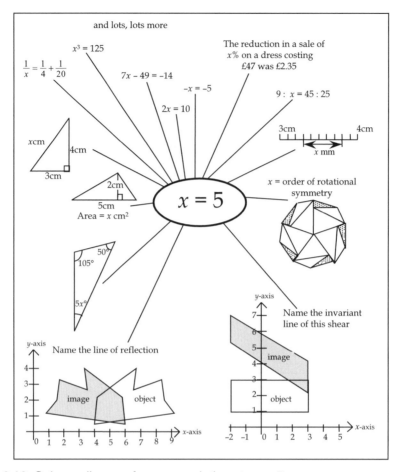

Figure 3.10 Splurge diagram for some solutions to x = 5

1. a) Using a protractor and a ruler draw a triangle with angles of 30°, 60°
   and 90° with one side measuring 9cm.
   b) Using a pair of compasses and a ruler draw a triangle with angles of 30°,
   60° and 90° with one side measuring 9cm.
   c) Using a calculator, a ruler and a 45° set-square draw a triangle with angles
   of 30°, 60° and 90° with one side measuring 9cm.
   d) Using LOGO draw a triangle with angles of 30°, 60° and 90° with one side
   measuring 9cm.
   e) Draw a triangle with angles of 30°, 60° and 90° with one side measuring
   9cm on a balloon.

Altering the resources that the pupils are expected to use changes the
mathematics considerably; in this instance from measuring angles, to construction
work, to knowledge of trigonometry to … How do you draw a triangle on curved

space? If you are aware of the possibilities in the mathematics you can create different activities for the different range of pupil attainment in your class.

Questions 2 and 3 are similar in kind. To answer the first in each set requires the solver to know about the mathematics. In 2a, for example, the solver needs to know about powers, substitution and plotting coordinate points. Altering the resources enables the graph to be created immediately and it is vital that another purpose is given to pupils for drawing the graph in the first place (e.g. change the power and see what happens, change the added constant and see what happens).

2. a) Draw the graph of $y = x^3 + 7x$ using pencil and paper.
   b) Draw the graph of $y = x^3 + 7x$ using a graphics package (e.g. Omnigraph for Windows).

3. a) Find the first seven members of the family of fractions equivalent to $\frac{1}{3}$.
   b) Using a calculator that accepts vulgar fractions, find any fraction equivalent to $\frac{1}{3}$.

For task 3a, the pupil may be using an algorithm or remembering the pattern from the multiplication tables. In 3b the first stages may be trial and error: $\frac{28}{85}$ will not simplify to $\frac{1}{3}$, but later attempts may. If pupils are successful at this task you are more likely to be able to assess their understanding of equivalent fractions.

The final task in this series shows what might happen if the data on a worksheet is transferred to card(s). The activity changes. Instead of one opportunity for decimal addition from the worksheet, putting the fish on to cards enables lots of practice with decimal addition and ordering as well as the expectation that each member of the group will check the work of the others.

4. a) The following results (in kg) are from a fishing competition

	1st catch	2nd catch	3rd catch	4th catch
Liz	0.96	1.23	0.8	1.01
Jo	1.1	1.03	1.42	0.74
Sam	0.88	1.2	1.5	0.78
Sunil	0.91	1.04	1.37	1.32

Find the total weight of fish caught by each competitor.
Who wins each round? Who has won first prize?

4 b) Design 20 (or more) fish cards, with pictures on one side and weights written on the back. Organise the pupils in a fishing competition. In groups of four they each have to pick four fish in turn, find the total weight of their own catch and declare a winner. This activity can be repeated many times.

Change the format

Many questions in mathematics come in different formats. It is worth considering these and collecting ideas together so that you can exploit them in your teaching.

Figure 3.11 shows different formats related to the question $4x + 2 = 10$. All of these can be found in different textbooks. Seeing them all together helps to realise the choices that are available.

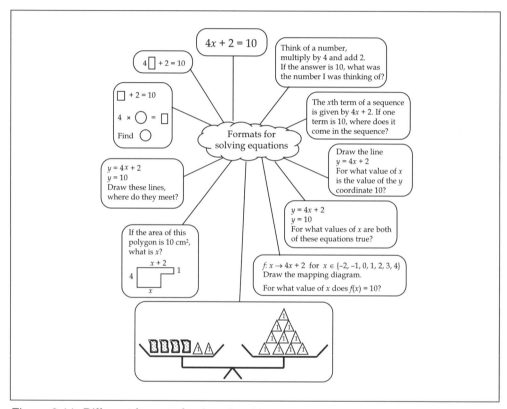

Figure 3.11 Different formats for $4x + 2 = 10$

Calculating the sum of the first n integers can also be presented in many different formats. In fact the resulting 'triangle numbers', as they are often called, appear in many guises throughout secondary school mathematics. Changing the format of the presentation affects the apparent level of the mathematics. For example it could be given as a set of sums to calculate.

$$1 + 2 =$$
$$1 + 2 + 3 =$$
$$1 + 2 + 3 + 4 =$$
$$1 + 2 + 3 + 4 + 5 =$$
$$1 + 2 + 3 + 4 + 5 + \ldots + 19 + 20 =$$
$$1 + 2 + 3 + 4 + 5 + \ldots + 99 + 100 =$$

It could be presented using a picture, as in Figure 3.12, or using cubes, to provide a different format for the numbers, but the context also alters in that the calculation is not as explicit. Figure 3.12 shows a picture of the first four cube staircases.

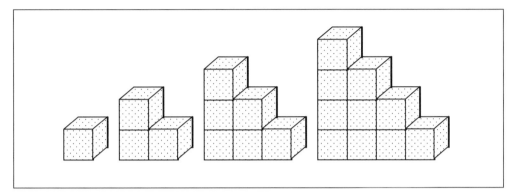

Figure 3.12 Cube staircases

The questions often asked here are: 'How many cubes are there in each of the staircases?', 'How many cubes will be in the fifth, eighth, tenth staircase?' and 'What about the hundredth?' The relationships between the numbers may be made clearer by the manipulation of models, because models can be joined together. The relationship of the numbers to the staircase may become less apparent as you work with larger numbers, with the process of abstraction becoming more important.

The problem can appear to be much more difficult if it is put into the context of the notation used in the advanced level mathematics classroom (Figure 3.13).

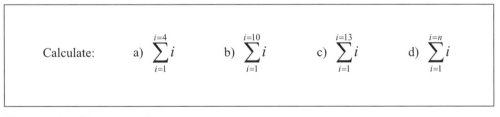

Calculate: a) $\sum_{i=1}^{i=4} i$ b) $\sum_{i=1}^{i=10} i$ c) $\sum_{i=1}^{i=13} i$ d) $\sum_{i=1}^{i=n} i$

Figure 3.13 Sigma notation

The mathematics is hidden beneath the notation and no patterns necessarily suggest themselves, although the addition is inherent.

The problem could be presented in a way which suggests no working methods or patterns of numbers:

If there are 30 people in the room and everyone shakes hands with everyone else, how many handshakes are there?

From old to new

Each of the four techniques described above offers ways of changing tasks. These are not the only ways, but you have to start somewhere. In later chapters we offer more ways of thinking about changing tasks, but we use these methods regularly. Chapter 4 takes a closer look at adding to and removing bits from a question. Remember, new does not necessarily mean better; it depends on the mathematics you want the pupils to be working on.

Removing and adding constraints

How changing, inserting or losing words can change the style of standard questions and allow you to create many more questions

The technique that we describe here is something that we have practised with our PGCE students over the past couple of years; many thanks to them for all their ideas. We were originally looking for a way of working with mathematical questions and altering them to include aspects of the first attainment target in the National Curriculum (Ma1), our belief being that this attainment target should be permeated across the rest of the curriculum. One way of including Ma1 in a teaching programme is to use a book labelled 'investigations', of which there are many on the shelves in our mathematics room. However, these often produce lessons about 'bracelets' and 'postage stamps' (which was not the intention of the authors) rather than lessons which are explicitly about mathematics. Also, there was an understanding that if 'bracelets' and 'postage stamps' were happening in the classroom then so, by default, was Ma1. This is not so! We're sure you have seen structured investigations that require little more than stimulus-response from the pupils, or ones that are so open-ended that it is difficult to tell what is happening.

As a consequence of this work on altering questions we had a rich source of new activities (and some to be put in the bin). Below we offer three sets of changed questions and we describe the way that we came to make the changes. We start each of the sets with a fairly closed question, but as we begin to move and alter the question the pupils take more and more responsibility for it. What is then required from the pupil is an explanation for the decisions made and justification of the solutions found. We are not saying that any one question in a set is better than any other question. (We are often accused of only wanting open-ended tasks.) We believe that the selection of questions is a matter of teacher choice for their pupils in a particular time, place and circumstance; to everything there is a time and a place. In Chapter 5 we analyse in detail the mathematical consequences of changing tasks.

A textbook question: using bar charts

We start with a textbook question on bar charts (although before you read on you might like to look again at the splurge diagram in Figure 2.3).

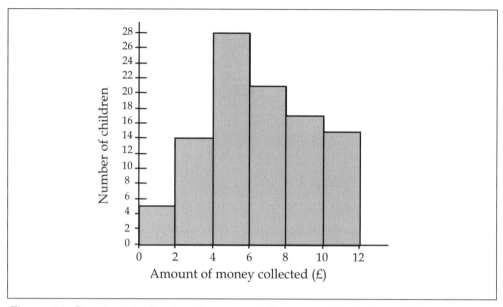

Figure 4.1 Bar chart 1, showing the amount of money collected by children on a sponsored walk

Version 1

The bar chart in Figure 4.1 shows the amount of money collected by 100 children on a sponsored walk (even amounts, £2, £4, £6, etc., were put in the lower intervals). Estimate the mean amount collected per child.

This question is probably a familiar one on the interpretation of bar charts. The sample size is given as well as the chart illustrating the data collected. The question asks for an estimate of the mean amount of money collected per child. There is one question and one answer. We will now alter the question by adding to it and/or removing parts of it to create new questions. For each question that arises there are implications for the mathematics that might be worked on by the pupils and we will discuss some of these. The whole spectrum of the subject matter related to bar charts will be explored.

The first change that we make is to remove the sample size; the fact that 100 children took part. The pupils have to make another decision about the mathematics. The pupils need to know that the total number of pupils is required in order to work out the mean. They also need to know how this number can be worked out from the bar chart. (In version 1 the 100 could act as a checking device, but how often do pupils check?) We also remove the words 'even amounts, £2, £4, £6, etc., were put in the lower intervals', which at the moment do not affect the solution as asked. So here is the version 2:

> **Version 2**
> The bar chart in Figure 4.1 shows the amount of money collected by children on a sponsored walk. Estimate the mean amount collected per child.

The pupils now have to make decisions to find the mean and how to interpret all aspects of the chart. It occurs to us that the second change about the lower intervals may make little difference to the original interpretation of the question, but the change can become a point of decision if pupils are asked to decide where to put results if:

> Five latecomers hand in £10, £9, £7.99, £9.99 and £10.01. How will the bar chart change?

We could change a word to provide some ambiguity; say, *which* average?

> **Version 3**
> The bar chart in Figure 4.1 shows the amount of money collected by children on a sponsored walk. Estimate the average amount collected per child.

Version 3 is a much 'bigger' question than version 1. The pupils have to decide which average would be a good representation of the data; maybe they need to find the set of different averages in order to make this decision. There is no reason given for finding an average so this might be an additional task in their justification of their chosen average.

The next version focuses on the mathematics in the diagram.

> **Version 4**
> The bar chart in Figure 4.1 shows the amount of money collected by 100 children on a sponsored walk (even amounts, £2, £4, £6, etc., were put in the lower intervals). Estimate the mean amount collected per child.
> What is the lowest possible value of the mean? The highest?
> What estimates can you give for the median and mode?

To answer these questions an understanding of grouped data and the use of boundary values to group the data are needed. The pupils are helped in this by imagining the reality of the data – they might imagine five people handing in £5 or five people handing in 2p.

Enough on changing the words; what about the diagram? Our first thoughts are about scale (version 5). The scale offered in the original diagram involves only a limited amount of interpolation, but by changing to a scale where the information is in fives (Figure 4.2), extra care in reading the data is needed.

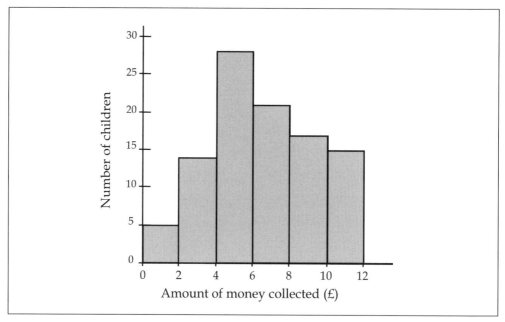

Figure 4.2 Bar chart 2, showing the amount of money collected by children on a sponsored walk

Version 5
The bar chart in Figure 4.2 shows the amount of money collected by 100 children on a sponsored walk (even amounts, £2, £4, £6, etc., were put in the lower intervals). Estimate the mean amount collected per child.

Having changed the scale what if the bars were altered or removed, as in Figure 4.3? The original question was about calculating the mean, so perhaps by changing the diagram a different aspect of the calculation could become the focus of the question.

Version 6
The bar chart in Figure 4.3 shows the amount of money collected by 100 children on a sponsored walk (even amounts, £2, £4, £6, etc., were put in the lower intervals). Add the missing bars so that the mean is between £6 and £7.

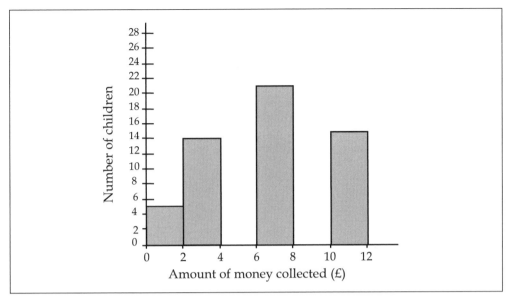

Figure 4.3 Bar chart 3, showing the amount of money collected by children on a sponsored walk

The question now demands a great deal of decision-making and input by pupils as well as justification of their solutions. If only one bar had been removed there would have been only one possible solution, unless we removed the number of children. Perhaps three bars could have been removed to allow for even more possibilities. Or perhaps this version can act as a prompt for pupils to design their own bar chart for 100 children, where the mean is between £6 and £7. An obvious resource for solving this question would be a spreadsheet. We will discuss changing resources in Chapter 6 and technology in Chapter 7, so for the moment we will just tempt you with the idea in version 7.

Version 7
On a spreadsheet show a bar chart which illustrates the amount of money collected by 100 children on a sponsored walk, so that the mean is between £6 and £7.

We thought that we had dealt with the words but what if the question is removed completely? Although the original question is about interpretation of the data in the bar chart, it is very guided towards the calculation of the mean. Making the question less directed towards a particular answer may encourage pupils to read more information from the diagram.

What happens if almost everything which labels the diagram is removed, as in Figure 4.4?

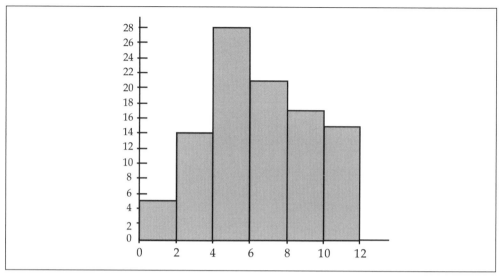

Figure 4.4 Bar chart 4

Version 8
What might the bar chart in Figure 4.4 show?

By removing the labels on the axes, a different aspect of interpretation becomes important: recognising types of data from a bar chart profile. What could vary from 0 to 12, with a modal group of 4 to 6? What data are possible? What data are completely inappropriate?

None of these versions have any real data handling purpose; they are only practising related skills. Can we create a purposeful context? If we are calculating averages we normally work from the raw data, but in this instance we want to work from the diagram. What about version 9, if it were accompanied by Figure 4.1?

Version 9
The headline in the *Evening News* was 'More than £7.50', and the first line of the article read, 'The average sponsorship money collected by each child was £7.80; well done!' The *Morning Post* stated, 'An average of £6.52 – what a collection!' Both papers showed the same diagram. Which paper got its sums right?

From one starting point there are now other possibilities that could be given to the pupils, each of which demands different aspects of mathematics. Some are still closed questions, whereas others offer an opportunity to investigate the relationship between frequency and estimated mean.

Two more questions

Here are two questions for you to think about altering in a similar way to the bar chart question. Over the page we offer you our own suggestions for changes, not for comparison or correctness but for extra questions to accompany your own.

The parabola

The question in Figure 4.5 asks students to draw part of a parabola.

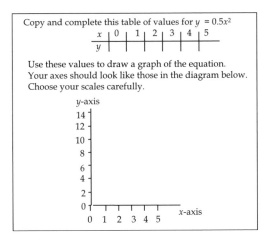

Figure 4.5 The parabola task

The rhombus

Figure 4.6 offers practice in using coordinates and recognition of a rhombus.

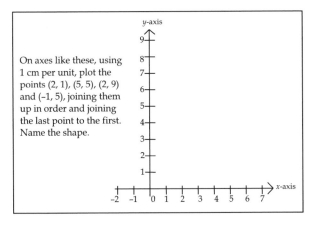

Figure 4.6 The rhombus task

The parabola

This question is a typical textbook question. The pupil has to follow the instructions given, although he or she needs to be able to interpret the equation and make decisions about scales on the axes.

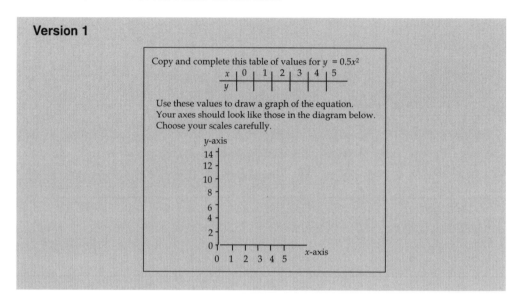

Version 1

Copy and complete this table of values for $y = 0.5x^2$

x	0	1	2	3	4	5
y						

Use these values to draw a graph of the equation. Your axes should look like those in the diagram below. Choose your scales carefully.

The first change that we made was to remove the table. As a consequence the pupils have to understand the notation for the domain and then decide how many values they will need in the table. They are involved more in the decision-making in the question and have to justify (and be responsible for) any decisions that they make.

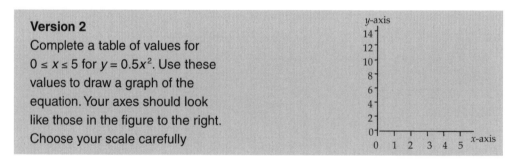

Version 2

Complete a table of values for $0 \leq x \leq 5$ for $y = 0.5x^2$. Use these values to draw a graph of the equation. Your axes should look like those in the figure to the right. Choose your scale carefully

The next change was to remove the axes. This means that there is no picture to guide the pupils in constructing a picture of the graph. No indication of scale is offered. Decisions have to be made about the axes and the scale.

Version 3

Complete a table of values for $0 \leq x \leq 5$ for $y = 0.5x^2$. Use these values to draw a graph of the equation. Choose your scales carefully.

What follows next is a careful removal of all the guiding instructions. In the next task the domain has not been given. The suggestion that a table of values is constructed has also been removed. Decisions need to be made about a sensible domain, as well as a strategy for collecting the necessary information.

Version 4

Draw the graph of $y = 0.5x^2$. Choose your own range of x values. Choose your own scales for the axes.

In versions 5 and 6 many more decisions are offered to the pupil. If the 0.5 in the original equation becomes a general coefficient, a, the question offers an investigation into the effect of the coefficient on the parabola. Generalisations are looked for from the specific cases, although the pupil is 'talked' through the strategy required for solving the problem.

Version 5

Choose values for a in the equation $y = ax^2$. Draw the graphs of your chosen equations. Choose your own range of x values. Choose your own scales for the axes. Describe the features of the graphs you have drawn.

Version 6 now offers the possibility of exploring the mathematics of parabolas of the form $y = ax^2$. No hints are given, and the pupil has to make all the decisions and justify solutions. (Here the possibility of using a graphical package or a graphical calculator arises and changes the nature of the question further, because of the speed with which the special cases can be produced. In fact this type of question would be much more sensibly approached using a computer or graphical calculator.)

Version 6

What happens to the graph of $y = ax^2$ as a varies?

The mathematics of versions 5 and 6 offers a stronger purpose to the task of drawing parabolas, because of the generalisation aspect, the recognition of the shape of the parabola and the effect that the change of the value of the coefficient has.

If you wish to focus on the table of values when you are using a computer, it would be useful to change version 3 to use with a spreadsheet. This focuses on the differences between the values of x in the table, and the number aspect of these, with the need to discuss the difference between the continuous nature of the function and the discrete representation given by the table of values (with the implications for 'smoothness').

Version 7

On a spreadsheet complete a table of values for $0 \le x \le 5$ for $y = 0.5x^2$. Use these values to draw a graph of the equation, using the scatter diagram facility. First use values of x with an interval of 1, then 0.5 and 0.1. What happens to your diagram? Why?

Creating a table of values, with the focus on changing the values of x, offers a different image in the spreadsheet context than those in graphical packages (versions 5 and 6).

The rhombus

Version 1

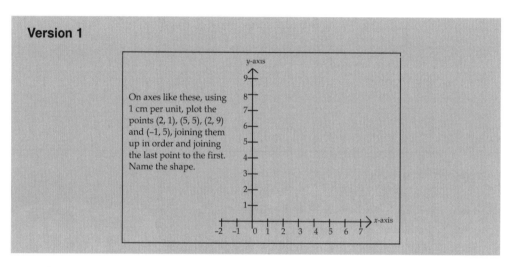

On axes like these, using 1 cm per unit, plot the points (2, 1), (5, 5), (2, 9) and (–1, 5), joining them up in order and joining the last point to the first. Name the shape.

As before, we start by removing the picture of the axes and ask the pupils to make more decisions about the range on each axis.

Version 2

Plot the points (2, 1), (5, 5), (2, 9) and (1, –5), joining them up in order and joining the last point to the first. Name the shape.

There is now the possibility of adding to this question. We can ask for some extra mathematics.

Version 3

Plot the points (2, 1), (5, 5), (2, 9) and (1, –5), joining them up in order and joining the last point to the first. Name the shape. Draw in the lines of symmetry. Find the area of the shape.

Version 4 arises by removing the coordinates of the fourth vertex from version 1. The pupils have to know about the shape, rather than relating a name to the shape.

Version 4

Plot the points (2, 1), (5, 5) and (2, 9), joining them up in order. Do not join the last point to the first. Plot a fourth point to make the shape a rhombus.

Having removed one point it now seems obvious to remove a second. If the pupils are given two points several rhombuses can be drawn. Once some special cases have been tried, a relationship between the vertices can be established.

Version 5

The points (2, 1) and (2, 9) are opposite vertices of a rhombus. What are the coordinates of the other vertices?

By only giving one point perhaps too many rhombuses can be drawn. But it is worth considering!

Version 6

The point (2, 1) is a vertex of a rhombus. What are the coordinates of the other vertices?

Version 6 could keep everyone occupied for a long time, but we do need to be careful that the mathematics our pupils are doing is appropriate.

The original rhombus had two lines of symmetry so this property could be used to offer a different emphasis to the question and make version 6 more manageable.

Version 7

The point (2, 1) is a vertex of a rhombus with $x = 2$ as a line of symmetry. What are the coordinates of the other vertices?

Considering two lines of symmetry leads to a particular set of rhombuses, constraining the solution to some extent.

Version 8

A rhombus has $x = 2$ and $y = 5$ as lines of symmetry. What are the coordinates of the vertices?

A strong mathematical purpose could be introduced to the task if we ask pupils to find the area of each rhombus. A generalisation could be sought as to how the area changes in relation to the coordinates.

Using a graphical package, such as Omnigraph for Windows, for versions 6, 7 and 8 allows plenty of experimentation. (The accuracy of the coordinates related to the symmetry lines can be checked by reflecting the shape using the symmetry lines as mirrors.) Additionally Omnigraph will calculate the area of the rhombus if you wish to approach the task with pupils who do not fully understand how to calculate the area of the rhombus.

We could offer many more suggestions, but you need to try the technique for yourself. Take a question and start altering it.

Some tasks to change

Below are two more questions for you to alter, followed by summary tables to show briefly our suggestions for alternative possibilities.

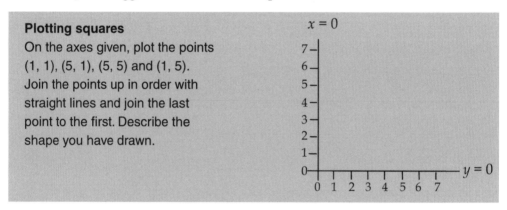

Plotting squares
On the axes given, plot the points (1, 1), (5, 1), (5, 5) and (1, 5). Join the points up in order with straight lines and join the last point to the first. Describe the shape you have drawn.

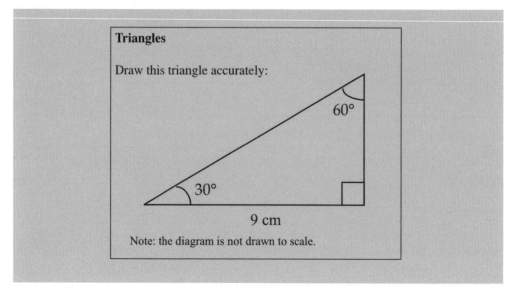

Triangles

Draw this triangle accurately:

60°

30°

9 cm

Note: the diagram is not drawn to scale.

Changing tasks

The removal or addition of givens to tasks offers a way of gaining new activities for the classroom. Some changes offer good ideas, and some do not. We are rather wary of the context for alternative 11 of the plotting squares question. We also know that if the task becomes too open, pupils can have difficulty. They need to understand how to cope with choices and become good decision-makers to tackle open tasks. We need to analyse the mathematical consequences of any tasks so that we can decide which pupils they will suit. Tasks that are too open for some may allow others to show their organisational skills as they simplify tasks in order to build up generalisations. Do not worry if tasks seem unsuitable when you first design them; you never know when they might come in useful.

The alternatives

Table 4.1 'Plotting squares' alternatives

On the axes given below, plot the points $(1, 1)$, $(5, 1)$, $(5, 5)$ and $(1, 5)$. Join the points up in order with straight lines and join the last point to the first. Name the shape you have drawn.	This question is about practising plotting points. Our conjecture is that most people recognise a 'square', and that this aspect adds nothing to the question.

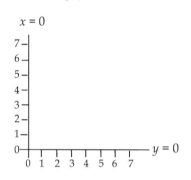

Alternative 1 Plot the points $(1, 1)$, $(5, 1)$, $(5, 5)$ and $(1, 5)$. Join the points up in order using straight lines and join the last point to the first. Name the shape you have drawn.	*Remove a given* All the information about axes has been removed. Pupils have to make decisions about the size of the axes and how to label them.
Alternative 2 Plot the points $(1, 1)$, $(5, 1)$ and $(5, 5)$ and join them up in order. Complete the diagram so that the shape is a square.	*Remove a given and change a given* Remove one coordinate, and 'give' that the shape is a square. This is still practising coordinates but there is a stronger focus on some properties of a square. However, there is still only one answer.
Alternative 3 Plot the points $(-1, 4)$, $(5, 4)$ and $(5, -2)$ and join them up in order. Complete the diagram so that the shape is a square.	*Make the givens more demanding* The pupils now have to work with negative coordinates.
Alternative 4 Draw the square(s) for which one side is defined by joining, by a straight line, the points $(-2, 2)$ and $(3, 2)$.	*Remove a given and add information* Removing another given creates some ambiguity but this is managed by some extra information. Additionally, there is now more than one answer.
Alternative 5 Draw the square(s) with the points $(-2, 2)$ and $(3, 2)$ lying on one side.	*Remove a given* This is like Alternative 4, but with the ambiguity retained - there are lots of answers. Justification and explanation become an important aspect of the solutions.
Alternative 6 Draw the square(s) with the points $(1, 4)$ and $(-1, 4)$ as vertices.	*Remove givens* There is more than one answer as only two points remain to define the shape. Pupils need to be aware of alternative orientations of the square.
Alternative 7 Draw square(s) with $(1, 1)$ and $(1, 4)$ on one side.	*Change a given* The vertices have been exchanged for sides. There are lots of answers. Here the coordinates are 'on' the sides of the square rather than being the vertices.
Alternative 8 Draw the square(s) which have the point $(1, 1)$ as a vertex.	*Remove a given* Only one coordinate remains. This has lots of answers, and decisions about generality may be necessary.

Alternative 9
Plot the points (1, 1), (4, -2), (7, 1), (-2, -2), (1, -2), (-2, 1), (4, 4), (-2, 4) and (1, 4). Draw as many squares as you can with four of the plotted points as vertices.

Add givens
More points are added, offering extra practice in plotting coordinates and finding and drawing squares.

Alternative 10
Plot the points (1, 1), (5, 1), (5, 5) and (1, 5). Join the points up in order using straight lines and join the last point to the first. Plot six more points so that you can draw more squares.

Add a given
An extra instruction is given, which requires some strategic thinking from pupils. A purpose has been created.

Alternative 11
On the plan of a holiday camp, draw the square recreation area, three of whose corners are given by the coordinates (1, 1), (5, 1) and (5, 5).

Add a given
Create a 'context'.

Table 4.2 'Triangle task' alternatives

Draw this triangle accurately:

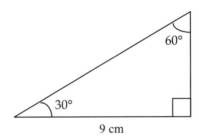

Note: the diagram is not drawn to scale.

Alternative 1
Draw triangles with angles 30°, 60°, 90° and one side of 9cm.

Remove a given
Neither the diagram nor the position of the side of 9cm is given. Three diagrams are possible.

Alternative 2
Draw triangles with angles 30°, 60°, 90° and one side of 9m.

Change a given
The length of the side is changed from centimetres to metres. The scale of the problem changes.

Alternative 3
Draw triangles with angles 30°, 60°, 90°.

Remove a given
The length is removed, and now many different triangles can be drawn. The mathematics now moves to ideas of similarity.

Alternative 4
Draw triangles with angles 30°, 60°, 90°. Measure and label the length of the shortest side.

Add a given
Instructions are added to focus on the lengths of sides. Ratio and similarity or Pythagoras's theorem could now be explored.

Alternative 5
Draw triangles with one angle of 30°.

Remove givens
The sizes of the other angles are removed. The focus is now on the angle sum of a triangle.

Alternative 6
Draw triangles with angles 30°, 60°, 80°.

Change a given
One of the angles is changed and the task is now impossible, with an even stronger focus on the angle sum of a triangle.

CHAPTER 5

The consequences of changing a task

How, by analysing the different versions of a question, you can become more aware of the mathematical possibilities

In Chapter 4 we described the changes that could be made to a question to create new tasks. In this chapter we take all of the changes to the rhombus task (and some of the versions of the other tasks) and consider the consequences for the teacher, the learner and the mathematics. The style and wording of a question can limit or extend choices for the teacher and for the learner and we analyse the resulting consequences for the mathematics. The focus on choices raises some interesting issues. By slightly altering a fairly common textbook task you can provide alternatives which involve pupils in different degrees of making decisions, leaving the teacher with the decision about which is the appropriate task for a particular lesson. The analysis of the decision-making involved in a particular version of a task helps us to:

- recognise the mathematics hidden in the question;
- realise the possible stumbling blocks in what may seem to be a fairly straightforward question;
- realise the possibilities available to us as teachers.

However, we do believe that it is impossible to say what a pupil will learn as a consequence of sitting in a lesson and working on a particular task. 'Teaching takes place in time: learning takes place over time' (Mason 1991). The analysis of the mathematics within a task can only offer a description of the potential for learning. We detail these as opportunities for learning mathematics. Only the interaction between the learner, the teacher and the mathematics can help to maximise the potential of any mathematical task.

Analysing choice and the potential for mathematics

Some of the decisions pupils and teachers face when approaching tasks are not necessarily related to the mathematics content. Making decisions about whether to read the question or how to read the question are skills commonly needed by pupils for many subjects, but remembering conventions, such as the order of reading coordinates, belongs to the subject and such tests of memory will depend on the task itself. Other aspects, such as explaining and justifying the mathematics, are not inherent in many mathematics tasks, but as teachers we should be encouraging their presence at every opportunity.

Question 1: Coordinates and the rhombus

Version 1

In Chapter 4 we gave the following textbook style question, from which we created alternatives.

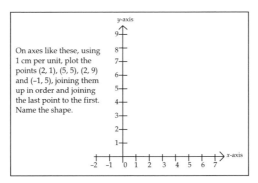

Figure 5.1 The rhombus task first shown in Figure 4.6

Pupils have to make decisions on whether or not they read the question. They may only scan the task and just read the coordinates. They may even ask the teacher what to do, rather than work it out for themselves. The learned helplessness we create in classrooms can stem from failure to work on the skill of reading and interpreting the question. How do pupils read the question? What skills and techniques have they been offered? How do they make sense of the data and select the important aspects? How can the teacher help pupils to work towards solutions without doing the work for them?

The teacher is always in the position of deciding how much help to offer, but we draw your attention to this choice as a reminder that sometimes our help is counterproductive; it makes our pupils dependent on, not independent of us. Another decision for the teacher, inherent in choosing tasks, is how they will exploit the pupils' work on the activity once it is completed. Is the work marked, discussed or compared?

The pupil will have to decide where to draw the axes, on what type of paper, and remember (or work out) what '1cm per unit' means. The pupil, most importantly, has to remember the convention of 'across first' for plotting coordinates. Having followed the instructions, the pupil then has to choose what to name the shape from a selection of possible correct names. So even a very straightforward activity has many decision points. Is it any wonder, then, that our pupils choose to get us, their teachers, to sort the steps of the task out for them?

The mathematics the pupils will potentially be doing is practising plotting coordinates on a set of axes, which they have to copy from the diagram, and remembering an appropriate name for the quadrilateral (or parallelogram or kite or rhombus). The teacher will have to decide what names to accept, or how to encourage all the names to be considered.

The pupil and teacher choices and the potential mathematics for version 1 of the task are summarised in Table 5.1.

Table 5.1 Summary analysis for version 1 of the rhombus problem

Pupil choices	Potential mathematics	Teacher choices
• whether to read all the question or extract the coordinates and guess the rest	• plotting coordinates • copying axes and scales • recalling names of quadrilaterals	• how much help to offer* • which of the many different names to accept for this answer
• what type of paper to use		• what to exploit when the question is complete*
• whether to use the suggested scale		
• whether to measure or use grid lines		
• the order of plotting (2, 1); across first		
• the name of the shape		

* These choices, an intrinsic part of the teacher's daily decision-making, are implicit in all the analysis which follows.

This question is a limited one for the pupil in that either they can do it or they cannot, but it is good for assessing knowledge in this area of mathematics; i.e. for the correct plotting of points and for naming the resulting quadrilateral. The latter is an interesting teaching/assessment point in that rhombus, parallelogram, kite and quadrilateral are all correct names for this shape.

Having analysed version 1 of this task we will now consider the other versions. In what follows we will take each one and explore the possible consequences of the decisions that the pupils and teacher have to make and the potential mathematics of the task.

Versions 2 and 3

In these versions of the task the picture of the axes has been removed.

Version 2

Plot the points (2, 1), (5, 5), (2, 9) and (1, –5), joining them up in order and joining the last point to the first. Name the shape.

Version 3

Plot the points (2, 1), (5, 5), (2, 9) and (1, –5), joining them up in order and joining the last point to the first. Name the shape. Draw in the lines of symmetry. Find the area of the shape.

It is amazing to watch pupils of all ages grappling with drawing axes appropriate for such questions. Pupils often even want to know which way round to have the paper. In order to extend the pupils' decision-making, there are times when you will decide it is necessary for pupils to work on this aspect for themselves, by choosing to give them the task of drawing their own axes without all the information being given. The small alterations made to the original question have extended this particular aspect of the task (Table 5.2). The first decision for the pupils is how to begin. Is the presence of coordinates sufficient to prompt pupils to draw axes? Are they aware of the need to look at the maximum and minimum values of x and y before deciding how to draw the axes?

Table 5.2 Summary analysis for version 2 of the rhombus problem

Pupil choices	Potential mathematics	Teacher choices
The same as those for version 1 plus: • the size of the axes • the size of scale	• plotting coordinates • drawing axes • scaling number lines • recalling names of quadrilaterals	The same as those for version 1 plus: • supporting the drawing of sensible axes

Some of the decisions pupils have to make may be more explicit to them if they work on this version. For example, they need to decide how to draw the axes and size the axes should be and choose an appropriate scale. The task for the teacher is to help them to make decisions, not by telling them the answer to 'How big?' but by encouraging them. What information do they need? What, in the text of the question, will help them to make decisions? The potential for doing some mathematics and making mathematical decisions has expanded.

Sometimes it is important to find a bigger purpose for doing some mathematics. In art pupils might spend a fortnight completing one drawing, in English a week to create a poem. Connecting more mathematics begins to make sense of the previous knowledge that pupils may have worked on. Version 3 is a copy of version 2 but with some extra mathematics added. The shape has been constructed for another purpose: to practise symmetry and area. Subordinating some of the mathematics in this way might reduce the pupils' anxiety when deciding how to draw the axes, because this is now a more minor decision within the task as a whole (Table 5.3).

Table 5.3 Summary analysis for version 3 of the rhombus problem

Pupil choices	Potential mathematics	Teacher choices
The same as those for version 2 plus:	The same as those for version 2 plus:	The same as those for version 2 plus:
• the lines of symmetry • the method of finding the area – counting or calculation	• the lines of symmetry and the diagonals of rhombus are the same • the diagonals of rhombus are perpendicular to each other • the lines of symmetry divide a rhombus into four right-angled triangles • finding areas of triangles	• how to make the connections between lines of symmetry and the diagonals explicit • how to guide the finding of area

Versions 4, 5 and 6

The next versions build on version 2, with one, then two and then three of the coordinate points removed.

> **Version 4**
> Plot the points (2, 1), (5, 5) and (2, 9), joining them up in order. Do not join the last point to the first. Plot a fourth point to make the shape a rhombus.

Version 4 asks the pupils to position the final coordinate pair so that the shape created is a rhombus. Analysis of this question offers all the mathematics from version 2, but with the added focus on the properties of the rhombus. The question tells the pupil that a rhombus is required, creating the need to be aware of the properties of this particular quadrilateral (Table 5.4). In version 2, the pupils might finish the task by giving the name of the shape or not; identifying the rhombus is quite secondary to the task. In version 4, the task cannot be achieved without using the properties of the shape: lengths of sides; symmetry; or even that the diagonals cross at right angles.

Table 5.4 Summary analysis for version 4 of the rhombus problem

Pupil choices	Potential mathematics	Teacher choices
• to make any quadrilateral • to use symmetry, or length, or other properties	• properties of a rhombus	• what questions to use to prompt those having difficulty drawing a rhombus

Version 5

The points (2, 1) and (2, 9) are opposite vertices of a rhombus. What are the coordinates of the other vertices?

Version 6

The point (2, 1) is a vertex of a rhombus. What are the coordinates of the other vertices?

The slight changes to the wording in versions 5 and 6 extend pupil choices and add to the potential richness of the activity (Tables 5.5 and 5.6). Pupils are not told to plot the points, so their first decision becomes whether or not to draw a diagram. Some pupils may only need rough sketches, or even no picture, to begin to approach the task.

One of the major mathematical gains in version 5 is that pupils may come to recognise that each rhombus is related to all the others drawn. This can be generalised to recognising the existence of the general rhombus which represents the solution set. The act of practising the drawing of the many quadrilaterals also allows some pupils to stay with the many special cases and to consolidate their drawing of rhombuses. The process of specialising permeates the activity and these data might enable some pupils to generalise about these rhombuses. Pupils may possibly use symbols to determine the relationship between the coordinates of the shapes drawn and how this can be connected to the properties of a rhombus. The position of these two coordinates fixes both lines of symmetry. By connecting this to the properties of the diagonals, pupils may well be able to justify and prove their findings.

Table 5.5 Summary analysis for version 5 of the rhombus problem

Pupil choices	Potential mathematics	Teacher choices
• whether to draw a diagram • how many cases to consider • when to stop • whether to offer a set of special cases or to generalise • in what form to generalise	• being systematic • similarity and congruence • the difference between a particular set of results and a general rule for plotting the vertices of a shape • the relationship between the coordinates and the properties of a rhombus	• whether to suggest drawing diagrams • whether to suggest a number to do and whether to share the task between groups • whether to aid the decision or to ask questions to provoke pupils to continue • whether to share/collect data from pupils to build a better collection • whether to highlight symmetry, equations, angles and so on

Table 5.6 Summary analysis for version 6 of the rhombus problem

Pupil choices	Potential mathematics	Teacher choices
• whether to use symmetry, length, etc. • when to stop • whether to offer a set of special cases or to generalise • whether there are any special cases which might lead to generalisations • what becomes fixed as a result of knowing one point • whether to use algebra	• properties of a rhombus • generalising • controlling variables • sorting and categorising • using algebra • justifying findings	• whether it is a sensible question • whether it is a sensible question for individuals, or whether it should be a group effort • whether to discuss findings • whether to suggest using algebra • whether to suggest limiting cases • whether to demand justification and proof

So many shapes are possible in version 6 that the teacher may decide that this offers too much freedom, which will lead to chaos and little mathematics. With pupils who are more able to control variables, the task provides opportunities for them to set up conditions, which allow them to categorise sets of rhombuses with particular features. Examples are:

A If $(2, 1)$ is a vertex, and $y = 1$ is a line of symmetry, and the rhombus has diagonals of length $2a$ and $2b$, then the other points will be $(2 + a, 1 + b)$, $(2 + 2a, 1)$ and $(2 + a, 1 - b)$.

B If $(2, 1)$ is a vertex, and $x = 2$ is a line of symmetry, and the rhombus has diagonals of length $2a$ and $2b$, then the other points will be $(2 - a, 1 + b)$, $(2, 1 + 2b)$ and $(2 + a, 1 + b)$.

What if we were to consider the line of symmetry as $y = x + 1$? The other line of symmetry would be of the form $x + y = c$ (or $y = -x + c$) and finding the vertices may be more challenging. Is the other line of symmetry more difficult if the line of symmetry chosen is $y = 2x$? (How do you work out the lines of symmetry?) The mathematics can soon become very complex and challenging enough for your very bright Year 11 pupils. These generalisations might be tested by asking, 'For what values of a and b do you get a square?' The pupils could also be challenged to prove their assertions.

Versions 7 and 8
The next two versions create a deliberate focus on the symmetries of the rhombus, with special cases leading to the possibility of generalisation of the solution set; see B above. The generalisation for version 8 may be easier than that for version 7 for some pupils. It may be visually more accessible (its proof, using symmetry, may also be much easier). Teachers need to choose quite deliberately for which classes these tasks are suitable.

Version 7
The point $(2, 1)$ is a vertex of a rhombus with $x = 2$ as a line of symmetry. What are the coordinates of the other vertices?

Version 8
A rhombus has $x = 2$ and $y = 5$ as lines of symmetry. What are the coordinates of the vertices?

Each of the versions of the task offers different possibilities for the learner and the mathematics. They all include practice in using coordinates and in finding rhombuses, but different versions allow for different challenges suited to different pupils (Tables 5.7 and 5.8). If you analyse tasks in this way, you gain more experience in recognising the different possibilities. The more we analysed such tasks, the more tasks we were able to analyse and the more the opportunities for teaching and learning became explicit. Analysis of later versions of tasks enabled us to find new possibilities in earlier versions. Any task has inherent within it pupil choices and, as we have shown, small alterations may extend or limit those choices. As the choices were extended, so aspects of Ma1 and Ma4 became more obvious.

Once the choices have been identified we, as teachers, may offer tasks with many choices or just a few depending on the objectives of the lesson. As for the different versions of the task, we may choose one, some or none depending on the needs of our pupils.

Table 5.7 Summary analysis for version 7 of the rhombus problem

Pupil choices	Potential mathematics	Teacher choices
• whether to use symmetry	• properties of a rhombus	• whether it is a sensible question for individuals, or whether it should be a group effort
• when to stop	• being systematic	
• whether there are any special cases which might lead to generalisations	• generalising	
	• controlling variables	• whether to discuss possible areas and share them between pupils
• whether to use algebra	• using algebra	
• what becomes fixed as a result of knowing one point and a line of symmetry	• justifying findings	• whether to expect justification and proof
	• proof	

Table 5.8 Summary analysis for version 8 of the rhombus problem

Pupil choices	Potential mathematics	Teacher choices
• whether to draw a diagram	• being systematic	• whether to suggest drawing diagrams
• where to start	• the difference between a particular set of results and a general rule for the set of rhombuses	
• how many cases to consider		• whether to suggest a number to do
• when to stop	• generalising	• whether to share the task between a group
• whether to offer a set of special cases or to generalise	• controlling variables	• whether to aid the decision or to ask questions to provoke pupils to continue
	• using algebra	
• what role symmetry plays in the generalisation	• justifying findings	
	• proof	• whether to share/collect data from pupils to build a better collection
• whether to use algebra		
		• whether to expect justification and proof

Question 2: the area of a hexagon

We now move to a task that we have not looked at before, in order to analyse the effect of changes to the mathematics and the potential for choice. This question is very similar to one used in Chapter 3, but this time the focus is on area. Version 1 is the question as it came out of a textbook.

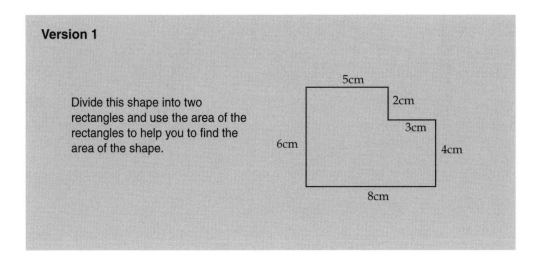

Version 1

Divide this shape into two rectangles and use the area of the rectangles to help you to find the area of the shape.

5cm
2cm
3cm
6cm
4cm
8cm

The directions to the pupils are fairly clear and, assuming that they already know how to find the area of a rectangle, require only a certain amount of decision-making: they need to decide which measurements to use. The instruction to divide the shape into two rectangles might cause some problems: which two rectangles? Dividing the shape into only two rectangles may be efficient, but using three or four may be more comfortable for the pupil (Table 5.9). The difficulty with many questions is that we attempt to impose an efficient method before pupils are aware of a need for efficiency or of the fact that there is a choice in the way the area can be calculated.

Table 5.9 Summary analysis for version 1 of the area of a compound shape

Pupil choices	Potential mathematics	Teacher choices
• which two rectangles	• review of formula for area of rectangle	• whether to demonstrate which rectangles
• how to calculate the area of a rectangle	• conservation of area	• whether to allow other methods
• how this helps to find the total area		

We have decided not to give each of the possible versions we could, but to use as a contrast a version in which most of the words have been removed as well as two of the measurements from the diagram. The lack of 'noise' in the question might make it more 'friendly'.

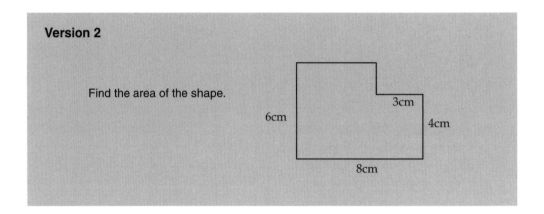

Pupils have to decide how to find the missing lengths, and whether they play any role in the solution. There is an assumption of accuracy in the diagram and many pupils will 'see' the angles as right angles, but some may find the lack of explicitness a difficulty (Table 5.10).

Table 5.10   Summary analysis for version 2 of the area of a compound shape problem

Pupil choices	Potential mathematics	Teacher choices
• whether to assume right angles	• review of formula for area of rectangle	• whether to demonstrate
• what method to use	• conservation of length and area	• whether to compare and contrast methods
• whether to draw an accurate diagram	• justifying method	
• how many different areas to calculate		
• how this helps to find the total area		
• whether to have more than one method in order to have a check		

The lack of direction means that pupils will have to explain their chosen method for solution. (This might be dividing the shape into two or more rectangles, but 'closing' the shape using the surrounding rectangle and using $(6 \times 8) - (3 \times 2)$ cm^2 might be an easier image for some pupils.) The resulting task requires more from the pupil than responding to the given direction.

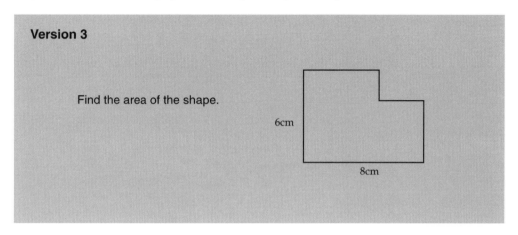

In the final version we offer something you will rarely see in a textbook. (What would the answers at the back of the book look like?) It has one major advantage over version 2, in that it offers potentially much more practice at finding the area of a compound shape. For us, it also offers the opportunity for a wider range of mathematics (Table 5.11).

Table 5.11   Summary analysis for version 3 of the area of a compound shape problem

Pupil choices	Potential mathematics	Teacher choices
• what method to use	• review of formula for area of rectangle	• whether to demonstrate
• whether to draw a diagram		• whether to support finding of special cases
• how many different lengths to use	• using letters to represent variables	
	• use of algebra	• whether to encourage use of formulas
• how many different areas to calculate	• justification	• whether to expect proof
• whether to use special cases only or whether to generalise	• proof	
• whether to use algebra		

The first new decision lies in choosing a length for one of the sides and considering the implications of that choice. This can be very difficult, because pupils are rarely given such decisions to make. As teachers we do this all the time, when we make up tasks, and this is one of the ways our mathematics gets better. For some pupils, encouraging them to draw a version of the shape on squared paper may help them to make a commitment to a length. The drawing on such paper may, however, inhibit the pupil from moving to the use of non-integer lengths.

In this version of the task, the opportunities for integrating Ma1 with Ma2 are strengthened. This also provides a version which allows for differentiation within a class: some pupils will be working with drawn images, some will be working on a wider range of special cases and some will be generalising and working towards proof. Version 1 then provides a task suitable for assessing the skills gained in working with versions 2 and 3.

Question 3: the bar chart

For our final examples for analysis, we return to some of the versions of the bar chart question from the beginning of Chapter 4. This task allows us to consider the mathematics of a different attainment target but also to consider the mathematical implications of using technology in our teaching.

Version 1

The bar chart below shows the amount of money collected by 100 children on a sponsored walk (even amounts, £2, £4, £6, etc., were put in the lower intervals). Estimate the mean amount collected per child.

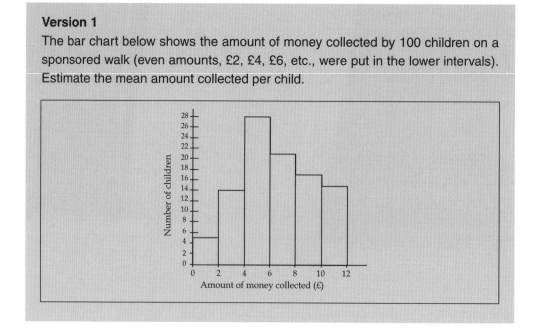

The bar chart is a grouped frequency diagram (sometimes called a histogram, but we prefer histograms to have frequency density up the side so that the area of the bar represents the frequency – that's a change to the diagram we did not do in Chapter 4!) Pupils need to be able to read frequency from the diagram, to realise that the height of the bar gives frequency and to understand the nature of grouped frequency tables: i.e. that data such as £0.45, £1.67 and £1.98 are represented within the first bar. To find the estimated mean, pupils need to be aware of the formula for finding the mean and the conventions for estimating (usually using the mid-interval). The question gives information about the ends of the intervals, so that £2 would be represented in the first bar and £2.01 in the second. This is a good illustration of how the representation of discrete data is complicated by the grouping process. The teacher needs to choose how much of this to consider when working with the class (Table 5.12).

Table 5.12 Summary analysis for version 1 of the bar chart problem

Pupil choices	Potential mathematics	Teacher choices
• how to read frequency • how to calculate the mean • what to use for estimation	• formula for the mean	• whether to highlight 'discrete' and 'grouped' • whether to offer checking methods • what estimates to accept

Version 6
The bar chart below shows the amount of money collected by 100 children on a sponsored walk (even amounts, £2, £4, £6, etc., were put in the lower intervals). Add the missing bars so that the mean is between £6 and £7.

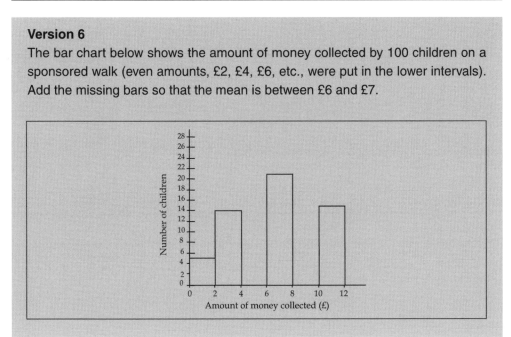

In version 6, where the bars are missing, pupils can work on the relationship between the frequency for each of these two bars and the final estimated mean. Pupils could be encouraged to find the lowest and highest estimated mean possible (Table 5.13).

It would be sensible for pupils to use calculators for the activity in this version. The relationship between the frequency and the estimated mean is more important than the practice of addition and division by 100. These multiple calculations are also prone to error, which would detract from the understanding of the mathematics. The task would probably be better done using a spreadsheet. Using a spreadsheet allows the focus of the mathematics to move away from the mechanics of the arithmetic to the effect of individual changes in the frequency on the estimated mean. A template could be provided of the frequency table (Figure 5.2) and the bar chart, so that the changes in the chart can be observed as different values for the frequencies of the two missing groups are added to the table.

As the solutions can be found by trial and error, there needs to be an expectation that pupils will explain their results; otherwise the mathematics of the task will be diminished (Table 5.14). Some pupils could be encouraged to move to an earlier generalisation by entering a formula into one of the frequency cells so that only one number has to be typed into the table.

Table 5.13 Summary analysis for version 6 of the bar chart problem

Pupil choices	Potential mathematics	Teacher choices
• what frequency values to use	• formula for mean	• whether to highlight 'discrete' and 'grouped'
• whether to use the total of 100	• practising addition and division or efficient use of a calculator	• whether to offer checking methods
• how to calculate mean	• being systematic	• what estimates to accept
• what to use for estimation	• finding the relationship between frequency changes and changes in the mean	
• whether to use a calculator		
• how many to do		
• when to stop		
• whether to generalise		

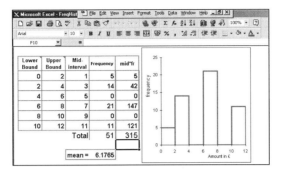

Figure 5.2 Spreadsheet template

Table 5.14 Summary analysis for the bar chart problem using a spreadsheet

Pupil choices	Potential mathematics	Teacher choices
• what frequency values to use	• formula for the mean	• whether to highlight 'discrete' and 'grouped'
• whether to use the total of 100	• practising addition and division or efficient use of a calculator	• whether to offer checking methods
• how to calculate the mean	• being systematic	• what estimates to accept
• what to use for estimation	• finding the relationship between frequency changes and changes in the mean	
• whether to use a calculator		
• how many to do	• justifying the relationships	
• when to stop		
• whether to generalise		

Version 7

On a spreadsheet show a bar chart which illustrates the amount of money collected by 100 children on a sponsored walk, so that the mean is between £6 and £7.

This task focuses on the mathematics of distribution and its connection to the mathematics of the central tendency, as represented in the estimated mean. A template could be set up, either with a frequency table (as in Figure 5.7) to be altered or raw data, which would give the exact mean, along with the frequency table. A version using the raw data to find the mean as well as the frequency table and related estimated mean would help pupils to focus on the connection between raw data and different interpretations of the central tendency (Table 5.15).

Table 5.15 Summary analysis for version 7 of the bar chart problem

Pupil choices	Potential mathematics	Teacher choices
• what frequency values to use	• being systematic	• whether to share results
• whether to use the total of 100	• finding the relationship between frequency changes and changes in the mean	• what estimates to accept
• how many to do		• what sort of relationships to expect
• when to stop	• finding relationships between the raw data, mean, frequency table and estimated mean	
• whether to generalise		

> **Version 9**
> The headline in the *Evening News* was 'More than £7.50', and the first line of the article read, 'The average sponsorship money collected by each child was £7.80; well done!' The *Morning Post* stated, 'An average of £6.52 – what a collection!' Both papers showed the same diagram. Which paper got its sums right?

Version 9 expects the pupil to use the original bar chart to find averages. There is, however, no indication of whether the mean, mode or median is expected. Both newspapers could have offered correct information, given that the value of the estimated mean is £6.52 and two or more children collecting £7.80 would give a mode, but other reasons could be given for different responses. The mathematics focuses on understanding the connection between raw data and the smoothing of the data shown in the representation. The 'purpose' has introduced a very different aspect to the understanding of data (Table 5.16).

Table 5.16 Summary analysis for version 9 of the bar chart problem

Pupil choices	Potential mathematics	Teacher choices
• which averages to choose	• finding the mean, mode, median	• what averages and reasons to accept
• how to choose 'raw' data for mean, median and mode	• the difference between mode and modal group	• how to offer suggestions
• what to use for estimation	• difference between raw and transformed data	• whether to compare and contrast pupils' findings
• what reasons to work with		

Some of the versions offered show a stronger emphasis on the integration of Ma1 with Ma4. Version 9 offers a way of looking at many different reasons to justify calculation and explanation of averages.

Conclusion

If we look at the potential choices for the learner and the teacher and the possible mathematics in each task, we come to know more about the activity. We are able to exploit the connections and the mathematics. If teachers analyse tasks in this way, they will be better able to decide how appropriate any version of a task is for a particular group of pupils at a particular time.

The more decisions a pupil has to make, the more explicit the processes of Ma1 become within that task. The analysis of the task not only helps us to find the mathematics but also to identify the processes the pupils may use.

Reference

Mason, J. (1991) Inaugural address as Professor of Mathematics Education. Milton Keynes: Open University.

CHAPTER 6

Changing resources

In which we tell about the consequences on the mathematics of changing the resources – some ready-made and some home-made

There are a wide range of materials available to use for teaching, from interlocking cubes to powerful computer environments. These different resources impact differently on pupils' learning of mathematics. All these resources have their part to play and each, as we shall show, enable different ways of both creating and looking at mathematics. An example of the consequences of fairly straightforward changes of resources might be plotting a graph. Imagine plotting the graph on plain paper or on graph paper or using a graphing package. Without doubt, different knowledge and skills are required to complete each task in the different settings. Would a pupil need to know all the different ways of plotting a graph? Well that is for you to decide, but to teach in a secondary school you need different possibilities, and analysing the topic in this way challenges your thinking about what it means to know about plotting a graph.

In Chapters 2 and 3 we presented a few ideas about the possibilities for creating tasks by changing the resources. In this chapter we look in more detail at the consequences of these changes for the mathematics. We leave you to consider the choices that this leaves for the teacher. We offer two different types of resources: ready-made and home-made. Ready-made resources are things like different papers, ICT and bricks, rods and straws. Home-made resources are alternatives to the textbook and worksheets – things like card games and board games.

Using ready-made resources

The splurge diagram in Figure 6.1 (repeated from Chapter 2) lists many of the resources that you might consider when planning for teaching about the equilateral triangle. There are different types of paper, different software packages

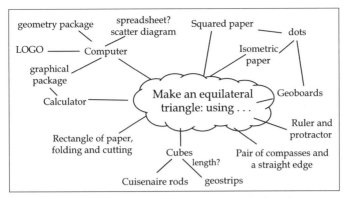

Figure 6.1 Possible resources for making an equilateral triangle

and different objects such as cubes and rods, as well as the 'normal' mathematical tools such as the ruler and protractor and a pair of compasses.

Making things like an equilateral triangle may conjure up creative, *Blue Peter* type energies, but it is not only construction activities that are affected by using different resources. Another splurge diagram shows resources for solving equations (Figure 6.2, repeated from Chapter 2). The resources shown are very similar to those in Figure 6.1, with the addition of using games to practise the mathematics.

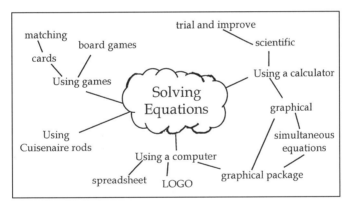

Figure 6.2 Resources for solving equations

As in Chapter 5, we will analyse the resulting mathematics as we look at using different resources for the 'same' task. Particular restrictions on the tools that you give to the pupils to use change the mathematical skills that they are expected to bring to bear to complete a task. A change of resources can create a different focus for the mathematics that is to be practised and learned. As ever, through this chapter you will read about the possibilities in and connections through the mathematics curriculum. To illustrate the effect of changing resources, we take two different areas from the curriculum: space and shape; and number.

The octagon

Each of the following tasks begins 'Draw a regular octagon', and the resources suggested are similar to the ones in Figures 6.1 and 6.2. There are a variety of ways of making octagons and in each of these versions the task constrains the learner by the suggestion for the resources. These constraints affect the particular mathematics that the pupils have to recall and work on. A point to consider here is that not all the questions are essentially about octagons; making an octagon is sometimes a means to other mathematical purposes. We will deal first with the 'normal' tools available in classrooms for constructions. Here is the first version:

> **Version 1**
> Draw a regular octagon using a sheet of A4 paper, a pair of compasses, a protractor and a ruler.

This task is mainly about the octagon. Solutions rely on knowing about some of the properties of an octagon. There is a choice of method for drawing this shape with these tools: either inside a circle or drawing one side at a time. The skills and knowledge required are:

- knowing that a regular octagon has eight equal angles and eight equal sides;
- knowing that the construction uses the division of a circle into eight sectors;
- division of 360 by 8;
- drawing a circle;
- measuring angles.

We now play with version 1 by taking away some of the givens. Version 2 gets rid of the protractor, which means that the angles cannot be measured.

> **Version 2**
> Draw a regular octagon using a sheet of A4 paper, a pair of compasses and a ruler.

The most likely solution might be to construct a sector which is an eighth of a circle using the compasses to create the 45° angle; that is, construct a right angle and bisect it (where the construction depends on a knowledge of equal arcs and the role of loci).

Version 3 is a slight variation on version 2, but with a seemingly harmless additional constraint: the request that the side of the octagon is 5cm.

> **Version 3**
> Draw a regular octagon of side 5cm using a sheet of A4 paper, a pair of compasses and a ruler.

This is really not so harmless. It can be achieved step-by-step by drawing a 5cm line, constructing a 135° angle at each end, and then drawing the next sides. An easier alternative might be to use the construction in version 2 and then by trial and error use concentric circles or similar triangles to create the correct size of the octagon (an obvious method to explore with a geometry package). The more mathematically demanding solution, for this type of construction, would be to use trigonometry and a calculator to work out the size of the radius: in this instance 2.5sin 22.5°.

The use of different papers is very common in mathematics departments so a version using these is given next. Imagine the previous three versions but with square or triangular dotted paper. How will this affect the construction?

Version 4
Draw a regular octagon using square and triangular dotted paper, a pair of compasses, a protractor and a ruler as necessary.

The knowledge needed here might involve the role of the isosceles triangles in the octagon. Depending on the type of paper an angle of 45° can be used to make the isosceles triangle needed for the octagon and then the isosceles triangle can be repeated to create the regular polygon. The triangular dotted paper should be rejected by the pupil as unhelpful, as its connection to angles of 60° is more likely to confuse. It may be that the pupil will be attracted into the error of drawing a regular hexagon when offered such a choice of paper.

Now let's look at the use of ICT. The introduction of computer technology does not immediately change the mathematics. In fact, to use software such as Cabri-Géomètre or The Geometer's Sketchpad requires a good knowledge of geometry, although the play is more immediate and many drawings can be experimented with, without frustration as mistakes are quickly removed.

Version 5
Draw a regular octagon using a geometry package.

The focus remains on the construction, but given the speed of working in such an environment you could change the task so that pupils have to find three alternative methods of construction and to compare the efficiency of such constructions. This would combine the mathematics of versions 1–3.

The next choice of software is LOGO.

Version 6
Draw a regular octagon using LOGO.

The focus is on the dynamic properties of the octagon, in particular:

- external angles of an octagon;
- the 'eightness', in order to use the REPEAT instruction.

The task could also lead to a generalisation of the construction of any regular polygon.

Having used the obvious geometry packages the question arises as to whether you could use a graphical package (such as Omnigraph for Windows) or a spreadsheet. Does it make sense to use something so seemingly removed from the geometry of the task, although Omnigraph does have a command to draw regular polygons. What are the advantages of graphical packages? Well graphical packages can draw lines of Cartesian equations very quickly. An octagon is made up of straight lines, so the intersection of straight lines could enclose an octagon, which leads to the next possibility. With a higher GCSE group you might like to practise the construction of a regular octagon using interrelated straight lines.

Version 7

Draw a regular octagon using a graphical package by drawing straight lines so that the intersections form the octagon.

The angles may be easy to achieve, given an understanding of gradient, but it may be more difficult to convince others about the length of the sides being the same. Are they in Figure 6.3?

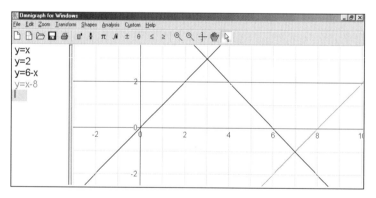

Figure 6.3 A screen dump from Omnigraph for Windows

Does having the x- and y-axes as lines of symmetry help? Is this too difficult? It might be easier to use the transformations that are available in Omnigraph. Draw a line segment and then reflect, rotate or translate it and/or its images to form the eight sides.

What about a spreadsheet? Might this be used to construct an octagon? The first thing to do is to ask the question and then be sufficiently bold not to reject it outright. The intersecting straight lines in version 7 make us think about coordinates and plotting points and scatter graphs and then spreadsheets. So it might be possible.

Version 8

Draw a regular octagon by plotting points using a spreadsheet.

You might first begin with trial and error, typing in some coordinates and getting a graph using the scatter diagram facility of a spreadsheet. You could drag some points (Figure 6.4). But then you might want to convince others that your shape is regular! How could you do this?

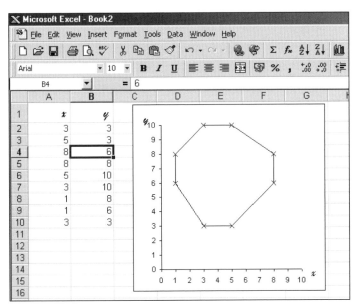

Figure 6.4 Plotting an octagon using a spreadsheet

It is worth pausing to play with the mathematics in this question. The trigonometry aspect of construction can be highlighted by asking for the task to be done using trigonometric formulas. But thinking about plotting points, the relationship between the vertices and the symmetries of the octagon could make an interesting question for vectors. What is the vector move that takes you from one vertex to another? Does the LOGO solution help here? The mathematics extends considerably. It is the type of question some of your gifted and talented pupils in Year 7 could be challenged by, before they are introduced to formal trigonometry or vectors.

Finally, change from construction using mathematical instruments or computers to something less technical, with scissors supplying the major change.

Version 9

Make a regular octagon using a sheet of A4 paper and a pair of scissors.

The main mathematics being practised here is the symmetries of the shape. To solve this task the pupils would need to know that:

- an octagon has eight lines of symmetry;
- fold lines can be lines of symmetry for cut shapes.

Have fun thinking! We will leave this for you to sort out.

It is amazing to discover the wealth and range of mathematics that emerges from exploring this particular task through changing the resources. It is also interesting to discover all the things that you did not know you knew about octagons.

Fraction diagrams

Drawing diagrams to illustrate fractions is a popular activity found in nearly all schemes and texts. As you will probably be aware, you have to be careful how you set such a task and be observant in watching what the pupils are doing and learning from such activities. Occasionally it can be more about colouring in than the mathematics of proportion.

> The children were colouring 'hundred squares' to illustrate percentages: 47 squares were to be coloured to represent 47%. Simon was busily occupied when he was asked what he had to do. 'Just look at the number and colour that many squares.' When he was asked what he was doing this for, he replied, 'To see if we can count'.

We have decided to take the activity of illustrating fractions to consider some different approaches and analyse the consequences of using different resources for the mathematics. The question we start with is 'Illustrate $\frac{1}{3}$ of . . .', and we will have a go at using the same resources as in the octagon activity. Here then is version 1.

Version 1

Shade this diagram to illustrate $\frac{1}{3}$.

The activity has a number of answers, all depending on the realisation that $\frac{1}{3}$ can be represented as two equal parts from six equal parts. The task then diverges from fractions to combinations: how many different patterns can be drawn, especially when the word gets round that you shade two out of six? However, even this task raises some issues about images for fractions. One of our PGCE students was working on this task with some Year 7 pupils. She found that although all the pupils were happy shading diagrams such as those in Figures 6.5a and 6.5b, fewer pupils were happier with Figure 6.5c as an illustration of the fraction, and even fewer with Figure 6.5d.

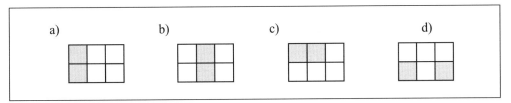

a)   b)   c)   d)

Figure 6.5 Ways of shading $\frac{1}{3}$

One explanation is that the resistance to Figure 6.5c appears to be due to the lack of obvious congruence of the shaded area with the unshaded portion. The four squares appear to be seen as a whole, an L shape, and it is difficult for some pupils to see this as two lots of 2 × 1 rectangles. For Figure 6.5d the fraction lacks coherence – it is not a 'whole' – and pupils are not using the relationship between $\frac{1}{3}$ and '1 in 3', the ratio 1:3 and its equivalent 2:6. Such analyses are part and parcel of every lesson and lead to a demand for alternative ways to discover the stability of a pupil's knowledge. It also reminds us that this proportion activity may have little connection with a pupil coming to understanding the number $\frac{1}{3}$.

The next alternative then is almost a repeat of version 1 but using multilink instead of paper.

Version 2
Use multilink to make some 1 × 2 × 3 cuboids to illustrate $\frac{1}{3}$.

This task gives an opportunity to make the link between $\frac{1}{3}$ and '1 in 3' more explicit. There is also the potential to connect to equivalent fractions, as there is something tangible for the '2 out of 6' representing the $\frac{1}{3}$. Making a diagram like Figure 6.1a, with two cubes in one colour and four in another, the most obvious $\frac{1}{3}$ is recorded. The cubes can then be rearranged to produce other patterns, the constant being the two cubes in six. The mathematics can also be directed to discussions of congruence and symmetry, because the models can be flipped and turned for comparison. Figure 6.6a can be flipped to produce 6.6b, so the similarities and differences can be considered.

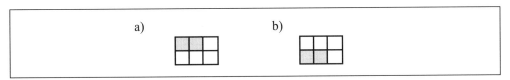

a)   b)

Figure 6.6 Congruent images for $\frac{1}{3}$ – reflection

Version 3 is similar to versions 1 and 2 but uses different shapes to focus on the '$\frac{1}{3}$ of…'.

Version 3

Use isometric paper to draw some diagrams to illustrate $\frac{1}{3}$.

In this version the pupils have to make a choice about the diagram to use (or we could give them the shape). The change of the shape of the parts, from squares to triangles, can challenge the image of the fraction.

What happens if we get rid of the constraint of given resources completely?

Version 4

Draw some diagrams to illustrate $\frac{1}{3}$.

Version 4 may have too much freedom, as no resources have been offered. Pupils can choose resources such as squared, isometric or plain paper and drawing instruments, but they may not be aware that this choice can be made or of the implications of the choice they make. The task is more likely to focus on ideas of equal parts and will probably be developed using congruence of shapes as in the squares and triangles (versions 1 and 3) or equivalence of area. It is in response to questions such as these that you will find out what the pupil really knows.

How might ICT help? Many spreadsheet packages have a paint facility which allows particular grid cells to be 'painted'. Imagine creating a worksheet with a particular size grid and ask the pupils to 'paint' $\frac{1}{3}$.

Version 5

Draw diagrams on a spreadsheet grid to illustrate $\frac{1}{3}$.

Because painting on a spreadsheet is faster than colouring using pencil and paper and corrections can be made more easily, more diagrams can be produced. The size of the grid can easily be changed, allowing more opportunity for generalising. It is possible to focus pupils' attention on the equivalence of fractions by using different sized grids and by recording both number and area (four cells out of an array of 12, nine cells out of 27, noticing rectangles with the same area) (Figure 6.7).

Having begun to think about spreadsheets the next illustration of $\frac{1}{3}$ emerged by looking at the other facilities in the software, such as pie charts. Circle diagrams are often used to represent fractions, and pie charts are circle diagrams.

Version 6

Draw diagrams on a spreadsheet using the pie chart facility to illustrate $\frac{1}{3}$.

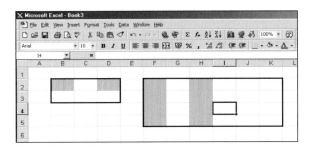

Figure 6.7 Colouring grids on a spreadsheet

The first question to consider is what the spreadsheet needs to draw a pie chart. You have to input data and you have to decide what kind of data to input. Different data sets would work and so a new aspect of mathematics emerges. For example {1, 2}, {1, 1, 1} or {1, 1, 1, 1, 1, 1} will all work: the spreadsheet will draw different pie charts. By changing the colouring of sectors (in some cases manually), you can obtain diagrams to illustrate $\frac{1}{3}$. The differences created by using different data sets offer different images of the same fraction (Figure 6.8).

Once you have drawn a few such diagrams, you begin to realise the infinity of choice available, and have an opportunity to look at different images for equivalent fractions. Using the data sets {1, 2}, {2, 4}, {3, 6}, {20, 40}, {100, 200}, {333, 666} and so on would give the same diagram as Figure 6.8a.

a) Data set: {1, 2}   b) Data set: {1, 1, 1}   c) Data set: {1, 1, 1, 1, 1, 1}

Figure 6.8 Pie charts to illustrate $\frac{1}{3}$ using a spreadsheet

Making your own resources

This section is slightly different from others in this book. Elsewhere we have been aiming to explain the process of recreating tasks from given tasks. Here the way of adapting tasks is to use the same material written on cards (for example the fishing contest in Chapter 3). When you have made cards, it is useful to be able to use them in a variety of ways. In this section we will detail some of the basics for creating card games from which you will be able to create a huge range of other ideas.

Making your own resources is often time consuming. How many you can make depends on the demands of a busy working year. If you do get chance to make some of the resources detailed here, we suggest that you laminate them so that you can use them time and time again. Over the years our students have used a wide variety of games to engage their pupils in mathematics in their classrooms. They make a great change from the textbook/worksheet type activity and even the most recalcitrant group can get involved as the mathematics is subordinated to the 'play' of the game.

> Two PGCE students were working with a Year 10, bottom set. Sixteen disaffected youngsters on a wet Friday afternoon, in a lesson watched by a tutor, seemed set for disaster. The students had prepared about 20 pairs of fractions and decimals cards. They divided the class into two teams, with each student turning the cards for one of the teams. They played snap for more than 30 minutes, with much hilarity, lots of good nature and none of the expected resistance to thinking that was normally a feature of these lessons.

The playing of games can provide plenty of opportunity for practice and can lead to discussion, since they are played in groups of two or more. And yes, they provide a definite alternative to all that writing. You will be able to assess the success of the task and the amount of mathematics happening by listening to the conversations.

Creating cards

Many mathematical activities have a matching element – a graph can be matched to its equation, a number to its factors – so cards can be created, either with the two aspects on the back and front, or as two separate cards for collecting together. Other cards can be created for ordering or sorting. For example, the fish cards used in Chapter 3 could have the numbers shown in Figure 6.9.

0.36	0.63	0.37	0.76	0.67	0.607
0.607	0.603	0.703	0.706	0.27	0.33

Figure 6.9 Decimal cards

These cards could be ordered or sorted by criteria such as 'a six in the hundredths place', as well as using them like a game for the fishing activity. You could adapt the cards for use in other games. This suggests an alternative for the fraction activity described earlier. If various illustrations of different fractions were put on to cards the activity could become:

Using the fraction cards, sort the diagrams which illustrate $\frac{1}{3}$.

By providing a wide variety of images for $\frac{1}{3}$ the pupil has to discriminate between examples such as $\frac{3}{9}$ and $\frac{4}{9}$. This may provide a stronger focus on the nature of the images and their relationship to the 'thirdness' of $\frac{1}{3}$. You can watch for understanding and you can ask why certain decisions are made, but you could also ask for cards that show more or less than $\frac{1}{3}$ and assess other aspects of your pupils' knowledge.

Resources such as question cards or number cards can often be used in different ways by adapting the manner in which they are used. The decimal cards above already have three uses, but you could also match pairs which total approximately 1, or differ by less than 0.3, and so on; we leave that up to you. If you are going to spend time creating resources, using them in as many different ways as possible seems sensible. The splurge diagram in Figure 6.10 offers some of our thoughts. A question card can be linked to its answer in different ways to suit the needs of the activity.

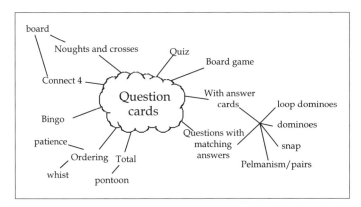

Figure 6.10 Splurge diagram for question cards

Many games and activities can be adapted for use in the mathematics classroom. Essentially there are two types of card game – sorting and matching – and then a number of board games, which use different rules for winning. Table 6.1 shows the different games that we have used. To devise mathematical activities, one way is to take a game and then consider mathematical areas that could be practised using the game.

Table 6.1 The different games we have used

Card games	Board games	Others
Snap	Snakes and ladders	Dominoes/loop dominoes
Pairs (Pelmanism)	Noughts and crosses	Hangman
Happy families	Connect 4	Taboo
Patience	Blockbusters	Countdown
Whist	Bingo	Bingo
Pontoon		

Matching: snap/pairs/loop dominoes/Happy Families

Snap and pairs you probably know about. Loop dominoes is a set of dominoes that can all be matched to create a closed loop. These games have matching in common, so the same mathematical topics can be used in all three types of game; indeed you can use any mathematical context where a 'question' and an 'answer' can be matched with each other. For example, common matching activities that happen in every classroom in the land are fractions to decimals, decimals to percentages and percentages to fractions. Other topics that can be used are equations and their solutions, angles and their size and sums and their solutions.

It is possible to make a single set of cards for these three games starting with the design as a loop domino set. A general design is offered in Figure 6.11. Cut them out as 2 × 1 dominoes, as shown by the shading, so that when they are set out they form a closed loop. The question is linked to its answer, which is on the next domino.

Answer 12	Question 1	Answer 1	Question 2	Answer 2	Question 3	Answer 3	Question 4
Answer 4	Question 5	Answer 5	Question 6	Answer 6	Question 7	Answer 7	Question 8
Answer 8	Question 9	Answer 9	Question 10	Answer 10	Question 11	Answer 11	Question 12

Figure 6.11 Designing a 12 loop domino set

By changing the shape of the cards and cutting each cell separately you have 24 pair or snap cards. This is where word-processing programs and spreadsheets become really useful for designing your cards (and storing your ideas).

If the dominoes are folded and stuck, so that answer 12 is on the back of question 1, you then have another loop game. Each person in a group has one card each. If you had the cards from the algebra game cards (Figure 6.12), one pupil begins by saying, 'I have $x = 7$. Who has $5x + 7 = 2$?' The pupil who has the

$x = 7$	$5x + 7 = 2$	$x = -1$	$3x + 2 = 20$	$x = 6$	$5x + 2 = 1$	$x = -0.2$	$10 - 2x = 5$
$x = 2.5$	$4x + 5 = 3$	$x = -0.5$	$6 - 3x = 12$	$x = -2$	$4x + 2 = 8$	$x = 1.5$	$10 - 2x = 0$
$x = 5$	$5x = 1.5$	$x = 0.3$	$10x - 1 = 0$	$x = 0.1$	$12 + 2x = 6$	$x = -3$	$4x + 1 = 3$
$x = 0.5$	$4x + 1 = 0$	$x = -0.25$	$5x = 1$	$x = 0.2$	$4x = 3.6$	$x = 0.9$	$2x + 5 = 10$
$x = 2.5$	$5x - 5 = 15$	$x = 4$	$4x - 15 = 25$	$x = 10$	$5x + 26 = 1$	$x = -5$	$3 - x = 10$
$x = -7$	$8 - x = 14$	$x = -6$	$5 - 10x = 4$	$x = 0.1$	$7x - 9 = -2$	$x = 1$	$4x + 1 = 2$
$x = 0.25$	$2x - 8 = 0$	$x = 4$	$3x + 1 = 7$	$x = 2$	$15 - x = 5$	$x = 10$	$5x + 3 = 3$
$x = 0$	$12 - 3x = 3$	$x = 3$	$2x - 6 = 8$				

Figure 6.12 A 30 loop domino set for equations

solution to this equation then takes their turn as they are next in the loop. 'I have $x = -1$', they declare. 'Who has $3x + 2 = 20$?' and so on.

The game of 'pairs' can be played with the cards face up (extra distinguishing marks on the back could be useful for some pupils to check the matching) or with them face down once the pupils understand the mathematics.

In keeping with the rest of the book we now say 'what-if-not' pairs but 'trios'. Pairs can easily become trios, where the object may be to collect the stages in a calculation; for example, trios which form part of a fractions calculation (Figure 6.13).

$\frac{2}{3} + \frac{3}{4}$	$\frac{8}{12} + \frac{9}{12}$	$\frac{17}{12} = 1\frac{5}{12}$

Figure 6.13 A trio of cards for a fraction calculation

A similar thing can be created with some algebra. The parts of an equation can be split up (Figure 6.14) with more than one way of collecting the trio!

$2x + 7$	$= 17$	$x = 5$
$3x + 2$	$= 11$	$x = 3$
$4x - 3$	$= 13$	$x = 4$

Figure 6.14 Equation trios

Your more mathematically able children could design these cards for you. Challenge them to maximise the number of possible different sets.

Take the pairs to trios, then take the trios to bigger sets. For example, you might add a picture of the graph to the above collection. Our advice would be to always think as widely as possible across the curriculum so that any set of cards can become as flexible as possible. One lesson might be about solving equations; later on in the year it might be about sketching graphs. Extending the trios to bigger sets leads to other card games. Happy Families is a game where you collect sets of objects. To adapt this game you need to consider where in the mathematics curriculum you want the pupils to match sets of objects. The topics already mentioned fit here as well. From the previous section you might use cards to sort diagrams which illustrate different fractions. Other examples include:

- equivalent fractions: families could consist of $\frac{3}{4}, \frac{6}{8}, \frac{9}{12}, \frac{12}{16}$ and $\frac{5}{6}, \frac{10}{12}, \frac{15}{18}, \frac{20}{24}$ and so on;
- fractions, decimals, percentages and division: e.g. $\frac{1}{3}$, 0.75, 75%, 3 ÷ 4;

- equations with the same solutions: e.g.
  $x = 7$, $2x - 3 = 11$, $3x + 1 = 22$, $10 - x = 3$; $x = 2$,
  $2x - 3 = 1$, $3x + 1 = 7$, $10 - x = 8$ and so on;
- shapes with the same property: the same number of lines of symmetry or order of rotational symmetry and so on.

Pupils can either play the game with such cards or simply be asked to sort them into like sets. You could also play snap or devise other activities.

Board games

Board games can also be adapted by using questions and answers to win positions. A simple board game, moving around a track, can become an algebra substitution game. Supposing you have a die with the numbers −2, −1, 0, 1, 2 and 3, a board (Figure 6.15), and a set of cards with algebraic expressions on one side and a table of values on the other, like the pair shown in Figure 6.16.

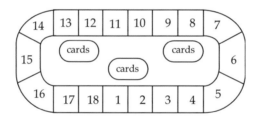

Figure 6.15 Game board

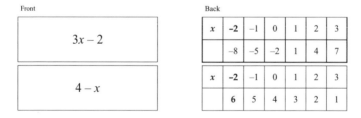

Figure 6.16 Front and back of a pair of expression cards

Place the cards in three piles, expression side up, so that players can choose a card before they roll the die (or, if you want to improve their thinking ahead, after they roll it). They work out the value of the expression for the value of x represented by the number on the die, and move that many places (clockwise for negative). You can decide how many times pupils have to move around the board to win (or they could move through particular squares – e.g. 6, 18, 10 in that order).

More traditional popular board games can be adapted with question and answer cards. For example, in snakes and ladders you play the game by throwing two dice, calculating the sum and moving forwards by that number. To play the game with question cards, the pupil answers a question correctly in order to move around the board and/or to climb a ladder or to stop having to slide down a snake! (You may want to adapt the board by adding more snakes and ladders.) The decision then is the form of questions and answers you want your pupils to practise and how the question design might change the focus of the mathematics. Bingo can be adapted using the traditional playing boards but rather than call out a number, call out a question: 'half of 56'.

Let's adapt another very 'simple' game: noughts and crosses. Different versions can be created depending on what you want your pupils to practise. These versions practise decimal subtraction and we show how noughts and crosses boards can be adapted to practise this for the classroom. For version 1 you need a playing board, some noughts and crosses markers and question cards (see Figure 6.17). The players have to select a card, work out the answer and then claim the result on the board with their nought or cross. You might like to have the answers on the reverse of the cards, or you could expect the other player to do the calculation to check. Like noughts and crosses the pupils might stay with trial and error for some time and they might repeat the same board on many occasions. (Remind yourself here how many times you have played the same game with the same rules – noughts and crosses, for example – over and over again. Maybe it is time to introduce this repetition into the classroom.) Pupils who are ready to work out a winning strategy will look at more than just one question, which is likely to develop estimation strategies.

Playing board

0.7	0.5	−0.2
−0.3	−0.4	0.6
0.3	0.2	−0.5

Win a cell by choosing the card whose answer is the number in the cell

Question cards

$1.25 - 1.75$	$1.73 - 1.4$	$-0.2 - 0.2$	$-0.4 \div 2$
$0.96 - 0.76$	$0.8 - 1.2$	$2.67 - 1.87$	$0.23 - 0.8$
$1.4 - 0.7$	$1.73 - 1.43$	$0.69 - 0.19$	$3.08 - 2.18$

Figure 6.17 Noughts and crosses, version 1

The alternative game is to give the number cards rather than question cards, which extends the skill level, and expects the other player to check the calculation (a calculator might be useful as a tool to referee) (Figure 6.18).

A third alternative is to use the question cards on the playing board. Have a pack of question and answer cards (question on the front, answer on the back) and deal nine cards in a 3 × 3 array to form the board. The player chooses a question to answer. If the answer is correct the cell is claimed; if not a new question is put in its place.

This use of number or question cards extends easily to four-in-a-row, or Connect 4, as well as the hexagonal board of Blockbusters.

Playing board

Number cards

0.7	0.5	−0.2
−0.3	−0.4	0.6
0.3	0.2	−0.5

Win a cell by choosing two numbers, subtract one from the other, you win if the answer is the number in the chosen cell

1.2	0.4	**0.2**
0.7	0.9	0.3
0.6	0.8	0.1

Figure 6.18 Noughts and crosses, version 2

All of these games offer opportunities for practice but the game environment often encourages checking and justifying of decisions. For some pupils the game ceases to be competitive but becomes collaborative in order to achieve the finish. In whatever form, these resources can be a vehicle for discussion.

Conclusion

Many resources provide alternative images for pupils, and their mathematics needs to be exploited. Expensive equipment, or that which you have spent time making, needs to be used in as many different ways as possible. Games and materials of all kinds have a valuable place in the mathematics classroom. They can be used to change the style of practice, to change the demands in a task, to change the mathematics being required or as an aid for pupils to think with. Technology offers us an even wider choice of resources for the classroom, but it is no use using old tasks without thinking of the implications of the technology for the mathematics that the pupils are doing. This is true for all resources. Drawing a graph without the use of graph paper or ruler demands a very different approach, whereas drawing one on a graphical calculator may need no skill. As teachers we need to analyse this aspect of any task as well as the content.

CHAPTER 7

Changing resources: using technology

How changing the hardware and software used can lead to very different mathematical practice

There is no doubt that technology will change the teaching and learning of mathematics, but what will change, when and how? It is crucially important that we develop new questions to ask, since answering the old questions with the aid of technology is often a waste of time. Focusing on old-style activities leads to myths such as 'calculators make your brain lazy'. In this chapter we devote time and space to ways of working with ICT, to use its power for the learning of mathematics.

It is true that for many mathematics teachers the use of computers is often timetabled for the term. This can mean that at the time of going to the computer room the mathematics topic may not lend itself obviously to using computers. But unless the use of computers is linked to the mathematics curriculum, the time is spent sharpening ICT skills – learning about LOGO or spreadsheets – rather than using ICT to explore and learn about mathematics. Stay with the challenge! The technology offers valuable practice for almost any mathematics but defining tasks requires some alternative thinking about the mathematics. If we connect work to that currently being done in classrooms, technology can be an integral part of mathematics learning rather than an add-on. And, because ICT offers a different way of working on the mathematics, pupils can gain different experiences to help their work on standard written questions.

A textbook question: arithmetic sequences

Take, for example, a very recognisable piece of textbook work on sequences:

Find the next two terms in each of these sequences:
a) 2, 4, 6, 8, 10
b) 3, 6, 9, 12
c) 100, 10, 1, 0.1

There seems little place here for technology. The machines can generate the numbers, but it seems a trivial task unless we devise new activities. The first job in this changing questions business is to identify the mathematics this topic contains, to find out why we are asking the pupils to answer these questions in the first place and then to connect this mathematics to other areas of the syllabus. The second job is to open up the possibilities within particular questions, using some of the techniques explored in earlier chapters. The third job is to discover the possibilities within the technology. The fourth and final job is to put all of these together to construct other questions and activities. The same health warnings remain. There are no right answers to any of this!

Job 1: what is the mathematics of the topic?

An obvious focus in this case is arithmetic sequences: mathematical ideas such as first terms and difference; inductive definitions; deductive definitions; different number sets; and other possible representations for the sequence. The splurge diagram in Figure 7.1 expands the possibilities for the mathematics in the questions above.

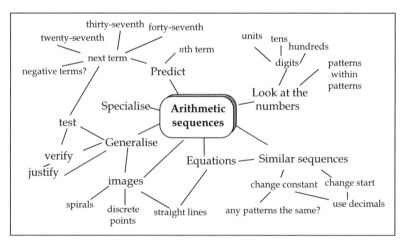

Figure 7.1 A splurge diagram for arithmetic sequences

Job 2: exploring the given task

Applying 'what-if-not' to the first sequence (see Chapter 2) leads to lots of questions and ideas to extend the starting task (Figure 7.2). These in turn give practice for the mathematical ideas within arithmetic sequences.

Having opened up the possibilities within the mathematics and within the task the next thing to consider is the ways in which the different technologies generate such sequences.

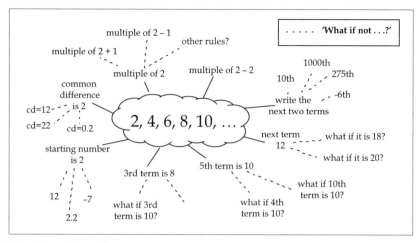

Figure 7.2 'What-if-not' for a sequences

Job 3: how does the technology generate such sequences?

Here are some reminders of the ways in which the different technologies generate sequences.

a) The calculator can generate arithmetic sequences using the in-built constant facility available on most calculators. For example, pressing '2' '+' '+' '=' '=' '=' '=' will create the sequence 2, 4, 6, 8, 10.

b) A spreadsheet program such as Microsoft Excel will generate sequences in two ways:
   (i) using formulas – e.g. 'A1=2, B1=A1+2' copied across the cells gives 2, 4, 6, . . .;
   (ii) using dragging – if the first two terms are defined, highlighting them and dragging across/down to copy them gives rise to an arithmetic sequence (if you have never played with this, try it and see what happens, some amazing sequences are produced).

c) LOGO can be used to generate sequences using recursion. Pressing 'HALT' will stop the procedure. (The LOGO used here is MSWLogo. Other versions will have different syntax.)

TO SEQUENCE :X
PRINT :X
SEQUENCE :X + 2   Use the 'STEP' facility so that things don't go too quickly.

d) Specific software might offer ways of approaching sequences. Check your catalogues.

It is now time to reconnect the mathematics to the technology.

Job 4: create new tasks

Using a calculator

As we said earlier the task for the pupils cannot be 'Find the next two terms'. This is a trivial task with technology unless your objective is for children to practise copying numbers. New questions need to focus on the mathematical structures and concepts within the definition of a sequence (Job 1) and emerge using the openings given by exploring the task (Job 2). Here are some tasks we have created exploiting the calculator.

> Consider the sequence 2, 4, 6, 8, 10, 12.
> When do we reach a term that ends in 0? Or 2? What is the sequence of these numbers? Why?
> What is the pattern in the units digits? How many elements are there in the pattern?
> How many terms are there to 100?
> Can you reach 71? How?

You could then change the constant. Working with different constants, such as + 7 or + 8, can help students to develop relationships between these sequences and their multiplication tables.

Graphical calculators can also be used to generate sequences, with the added advantage of many terms being seen at one time. The amazing Texas TI92 allows the same exploration but you can also start the sequence with n and see the terms $n + 2$, $n + 4$, $n + 6$, . . ., say, or start with $2s - 3$ and see the terms $2s - 1$, $2s + 1$, $2s + 3$, . . ., say. What an introduction to algebra!

Using a spreadsheet

Using formulas
Our initial idea to use with a spreadsheet exploits the starting number and the rule. Setting up formulas to keep adding 2 (Figure 7.3) generates sequences quickly and allows exploration of the changes which happen with different starting

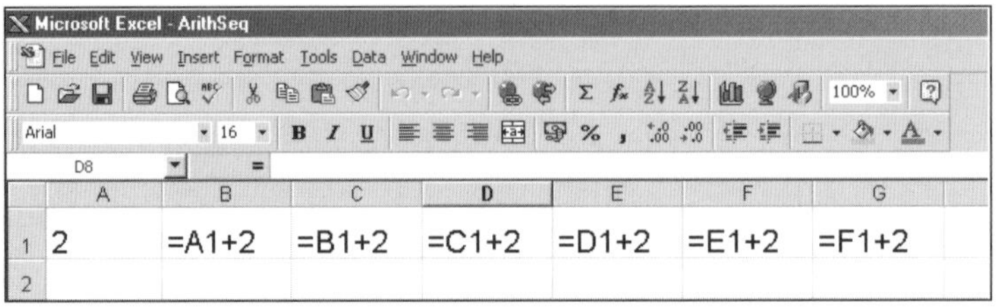

Figure 7.3 Spreadsheet formulas for 'add 2'

numbers: the number in cell A1 can be changed to produce different 'add 2' sequences.

Entering a formula into cell B1 and copying it across into other cells generates a sequence of any length you want. By changing the number in A1 the numbers appearing in cells B1, C1 and so on also change. It is easier for students working in this way to begin to accept that there are an infinite number of 'add 2' sequences, which are infinitely long.

Because all the terms of the sequence are available, unlike the transience of the calculator display, new questions (plus your own variations on these) might be:

> Consider the sequence 2, 4, 6, 8, 10, 12.
> Find an 'add 2' sequence with 10 as the third term, 20 as the seventh term (or 21.5, or −6 and so on).
> What starting numbers allow numbers ending in 0 to appear in the seventh term?

You may wish to have copies of all the sequences generated by changing the first number. This is easily achieved by copying and the purpose of recording now takes on a different aspect (Figure 7.4).

Most spreadsheets will graph the data, so you can explore the pictures of 'add 2' sequences with different starting numbers (Figure 7.5).

	A	B	C	D	E	F	G
1	2	=A1+2	=B1+2	=C1+2	=D1+2	=E1+2	=F1+2
2	7	=A2+2	=B2+2	=C2+2	=D2+2	=E2+2	=F2+2
3	-3	=A3+2	=B3+2	=C3+2	=D3+2	=E3+2	=F3+2

Figure 7.4 Formulas for three 'add 2' sequences

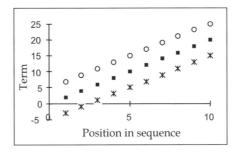

Figure 7.5 A graph of the 'add 2' sequences

The pictures of the sequence now allow discussion of discrete and continuous data and coordinate points. Why are the dots not joined? This may allow a move into equations of lines of the form $y = 2x + c$, and the connections between the number in the sequence and its position. Plotting sequences on a graphic calculator and then trying to determine the equation of the graph which passes through the points, is another way of exploring this connection.

Introduce a second sequence such as 'add 5' (Figure 7.6) to compare with the 'add 2' sequence.

	A	B	C	D	E	F	G
1	15	=A1+2	=B1+2	=C1+2	=D1+2	=E1+2	=F1+2
2	7	=A2+5	=B2+5	=C2+5	=D2+5	=E2+5	=F2+5

Figure 7.6 The 'add 2' and 'add 5' sequences

This allows you to ask new questions.

Create '+2' and '+5' sequences.
What starting numbers do you need to have the same seventh term? (This is a possible introduction to simultaneous equations.)
What common seventh terms can you have?
Can you predict the tenth term?

Exploration is a very important part of this process, allowing moving from specific cases to generalisations. Explaining and justifying play vital roles in these tasks. Working on a general definition (the nth term) can be tested on the spreadsheet by setting up alternative formulas or using trial and improve. Using the formula approach introduces ideas about variables and leads to algebraic ideas.

You may not wish to begin by using algebraic techniques with pupils but prefer to stay with the mathematics of the sequence itself. If so, the second spreadsheet method for constructing sequences is useful.

Dragging
A spreadsheet such as Microsoft Excel allows you to create arithmetic sequences by dragging across or down from two or more terms. For example, enter 1 into cell A1, 2 into cell B2, 3 into cell C3 (Figure 7.7). Highlight the three cells A1–C1, and move the cursor until it changes to a cross near the bottom right-hand corner of the highlighted area. Drag it across cells D1, E1, F1, G1, etc.

Figure 7.7 Dragging a sequence

It is easy to create the number patterns such as 2, 4, 6, 8, 10, 12, . . . and 7, 14, 21, 28, ... Creating sequences in this way may lead to alternative questions. Enter 5 into cell A1 and 11 into cell B1. Highlight the 5 and 11 and move the cursor to the square in the bottom right-hand corner. Drag it across to get seven terms (Figure 7.8).

Figure 7.9 shows some questions related to this sequence.

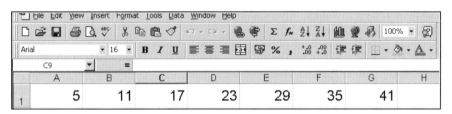

Figure 7.8 Dragging another sequence

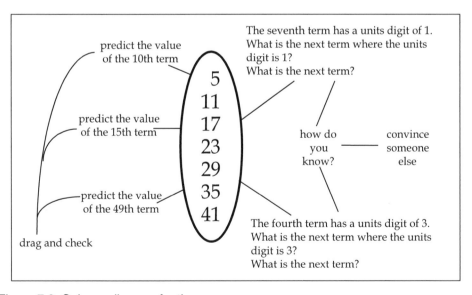

Figure 7.9 Splurge diagram for the sequence

Applying 'what-if-not' to this sequence leads to a whole range of new questions (Figure 7.10).

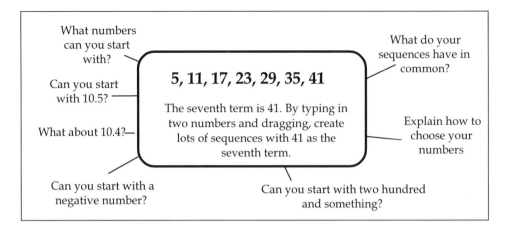

Figure 7.10 Splurge diagram for 'what-if-not' applied to the sequence

Using LOGO
The way in which LOGO creates formulas, with procedures calling themselves gives a different focus to sequences. Here is a procedure which uses recursion and produces the infinite sequence $n \to n + 2$:

```
SEQ :A
PRINT :A
SEQ :A + 2
```

If this procedure is entered, typing SEQ 2 will cause 2, 4, 6, 8, 10, etc. to be printed until 'HALT' is pressed. You will also need to use the 'STEP' feature or the numbers will go by too quickly. Mathematical questions which might be asked include:

Using the procedure SEQ :A
What different starting numbers can you use so that 10 is one of the terms? What about 23 as a term in the sequence (or 21.5 or –6 and so on)?

If you want the position of the term to be printed before the number, the procedure can be altered to:

```
SEQ :N :A
PRINT :N, :A
SEQ :N + 1 :A + 2
```

Using the procedure SEQ :N :A
What starting numbers allow numbers ending in 0 to appear in the seventh term? Which terms have the same digit in the units? Why? Can you have 23 as the seventh term (or –7 or 2.1 and so on)?

Just as the spreadsheets offer geometrical images for these sequences, so too does LOGO. The geometrical images in LOGO might lead you to explore spirals or ray diagrams:

SEQ :A	SEQ :N :A
FD :A RT 90	FD :A BK :A RT 10
IF :A > 100 [stop]	IF :N > 35 [stop]
SEQ :A + 2	SEQ :N + 1 :A + 2

Using specialist software

There is a lot of software available for mathematics. For example, COUNTER allows sequences to be generated by start and step sizes. Digits can be listened to, so sequences can be identified by the sound of the units digit, for example. You need to explore what is available in your school.

Drawing triangles

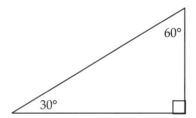

Figure 7.11 The triangle to be drawn

Jobs 1 and 2: an exploration of the mathematics in the question

The splurge diagram in Figure 7.12 explores the issues of Jobs 1 and 2 for the drawing triangles task (Figure 7.11).

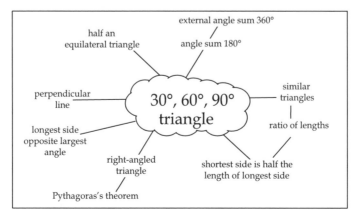

Figure 7.12 A splurge diagram for the drawing triangles task

Job 3: how does the technology draw such triangles?

Using LOGO

The construction in LOGO initially highlights the role of the external angles. Once this problem is solved the length of the sides and the relationship between them becomes the focus. This now offers a good introduction to the Pythagoras's theorem if different sets of results are collected. The challenge of nested triangles (Figure 7.13), could help with this or offer a way of discussing similar triangles and enlargements. Your more able children could use this to generalise their ideas before you introduce them to the theorem, while the others will be getting a feel for the lengths of the sides of triangles.

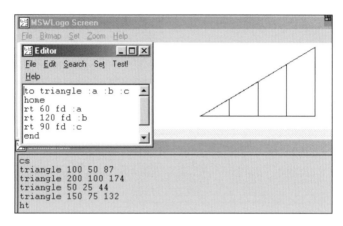

Figure 7.13   Nested triangles

Using a geometry package or calculator

If you are using a geometry package (such as Geometer's Sketchpad or Cabri-Géomètre, or a calculator like the Texas Instruments TI92), we can think of two approaches to the task (Figure 7.14). The first is to draw any triangle and mark the angles and then drag. The vertices of the triangle can then be dragged until the required angles are obtained. The mathematics focuses on the relationship between angles and lengths of sides as the shape is dragged. If you try this task, lots of questions emerge about what is happening to the angles as you drag the vertices, as this dynamic approach is not the usual experience offered when working with triangles.

The second method is to construct the triangle so that the angles in the shape are always preserved when the vertices are dragged. You could ask for a similar triangle or a congruent triangle. You really need to know your geometry to complete such a task. (The triangle might be constructed using a perpendicular bisector and the properties of an equilateral triangle.) By marking the lengths of the sides, data can be collected to aid with work on using Pythagoras's theorem or similarity. Using a calculator with such a package means that tasks intended for a short period of time can be considered, as there is no need to spend time in a computer suite.

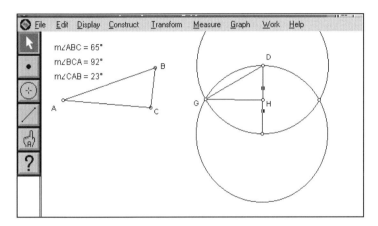

Figure 7.14 Two constructions

You could mix the two methods; a little construction with a little dragging. If you construct the triangle in a semi-circle and mark the angles (Figure 7.15), as pupils drag the 90° angle to obtain the others, the circle theorem itself is reinforced. Dragging point C preserves the right angle as the other two angles change. Labelling the lengths of the triangle would allow you to explore the connections.

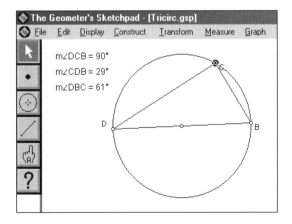

Figure 7.15 Triangle in a semi-circle

Using a graphical package or calculator

Using a graphical calculator or software such as Omnigraph for Windows, you could approach the task like the octagon in Chapter 6; equations of lines could be used to form a triangular region (Figure 7.16). Because no lengths of sides are given, the focus of the task is on the angles and the gradients of the lines. You need the axes to have the same scales – and pupils may need to measure their attempts. The challenge for your brighter pupil becomes harder if no sides of the triangle can be parallel to the axes.

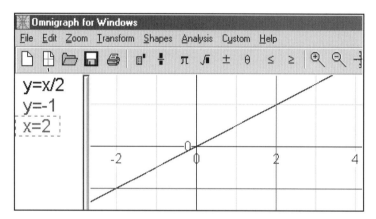

Figure 7.16 Using equations of lines

Using a spreadsheet

If you plot points with a spreadsheet, the focus is on calculating the vertices of the triangle, using trigonometry. The formulas which are available on the spreadsheet means that this offers a practical approach to using trigonometry (Figure 7.17), although you might prefer to use vectors. You do have to be careful of the scales on the axes!

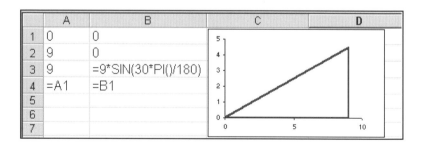

Figure 7.17 Trigonometric formula for plotting the triangle

How different does the calculation become if you do not use (0, 0)? What extra formulas are needed if sides are not parallel to axes?

Job 4: create new tasks

The task we began with did not seem to be very good material for using ICT, and yet by exploring the various aspects that the software offers, you can work on a wide variety of different mathematics from the same starting point. The tasks have been created by the differences in the software itself.

A tessellation

Constructing tessellations was introduced into the mathematics curriculum as a context for geometry, but it often appears to be a topic on its own, without any strong links to other aspects of shape and space (Ma3).

Take the task of tessellating 2 × 1 rectangles.

> Find different tessellations of 2 × 1 rectangles, where any overlap has to be of one or two units.

The restriction is added to limit the task; otherwise you could have very slight variations on the same pattern. Some of the diagrams you could have are shown in Figure 7.18.

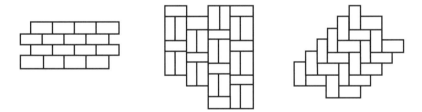

Figure 7.18 Tessellations of a 2 × 1 rectangle

This task could easily be done using dotted paper or graph paper, but we would argue that technology can actually restore the mathematics to the task (Figure 7.19), although you do need to choose your software with care.

If you use a drawing or painting package you are likely to be practising ICT skills and doing little or no mathematics. The same could be said if you were using a spreadsheet grid (Figure 7.20), where you format, copy and paste; these are useful ICT skills but not mathematics. Certainly, it is unlikely that you will be doing any geometry, but you could ask for the minimum number of moves possible, or the least number of gaps around the edge, to focus on a number aspect. How does the number aspect change if you change the size of grid to be filled?

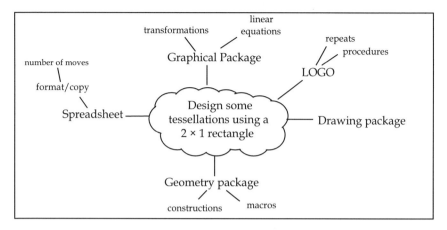

Figure 7.19 Splurge diagram for ICT resources for tessellations

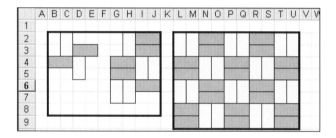

Figure 7.20 Tessellations on a spreadsheet grid

If you use the other packages you will be doing geometry! A geometry package focuses attention on the constructions and how these can be repeated. The construction of a 2 × 1 rectangle can challenge your thinking before you attempt to tessellate it (Figure 7.21).

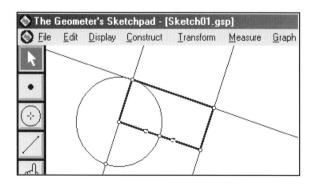

Figure 7.21 Construction of a 2 × 1 rectangle

The transformation of the rectangle by reflection/rotation/translation gives another perspective if you use a graphical package like Omnigraph for Windows. (You could use equations of lines, like the octagon in Chapter 6, but only with one type of tessellation.) LOGO gives yet another geometric perspective. How far do you need to move and in which direction to get the next shape? Is there a 'unit' of tessellation which can be written into a procedure? This would be a useful question if you are using Cabri-Géomètre or The Geometer's Sketchpad, because you can write macros. In fact, you can write macros in Microsoft Excel as well – that would highlight the 'efficiency' aspect.

Conclusion

The use of technology changes tasks – we need to question how this changes the mathematics. Spreadsheets will draw pie charts for us, so do we need to teach our pupils how to draw them, or is there a different aspect to the mathematics of pie charts we need to work on? Or should we use the spreadsheet facility to work on the mathematics differently, such as using the pie chart to illustrate fractions as in Chapter 5? The examples above show how similar tasks can be adapted to use the power of the technology. The calculator offers us a new way of teaching numbers: the computer offers us access to many other areas of mathematics. But if we use the same old tasks, we will just make our pupils lazy. We need to create tasks which exploit the technology but optimise the mathematics. We need to put mathematics at the heart of our use of technology.

CHAPTER 8

Changing resources: the learner

Where we explore what the learner does and how this can help us to change tasks

In Chapter 6 we showed how different types of resources influence the development of tasks. We considered external resources: ready-made and home-made. In Chapter 7 we looked at the consequences of changing tasks to use ICT. A significant, major resource we have not yet considered is the learner; we have not thought about the things that the learners themselves bring to the classroom. This chapter looks at some of the pupils' actions in the classroom and how using each of these as a particular focus can change activities.

What is it that pupils do when they are in lessons? They discuss, listen, think, solve problems, fidget, investigate, chat, doodle, write, chew gum: some of these we want to happen; some we don't, but accept and ignore; others we try to prevent from happening. Some of these things we want to deliberately encourage (in a mathematical context) because they promote learning. We have chosen six words to use in this chapter:

- talk
- write
- move
- listen
- imagine
- read.

We could use many others: drawing and recording we will include as part of writing; discussing will be part of talking. You might draw up a very different list. Some aspects we will not consider, because they underpin the whole of our planning for teaching. Problem solving, investigating and using mental methods are aspects of teaching where we always look for opportunities in tasks. Like thinking, we hope these are happening in most of our lessons.

We first offer two examples of the ways you might alter particular examples of activities to use the different human resources and then we will consider the generality of these attributes.

The first topic

Most planning for mathematics lessons usually takes mathematics content as the starting point; that's how most syllabuses are written. So for this look at creating activities we will begin with some content from shape and space: the properties of triangles. Next we will choose a resource for working on the properties of triangles, in this case a set of cards showing different triangles. This is a resource we have used many times before. Some of the triangles have right angles, some obtuse angles, some acute angles, some have sides of different lengths and some are similar triangles as well as the obvious isosceles and equilateral triangles. (You could include one or two non-triangular shapes or even a triangular prism.) Then we will take each of the words from the list above – talk, write, move, listen, imagine and read – as the other main focus for planning and create some activities accordingly.

Talk

Talk – purposeful and mathematical – is the focus for the first activity. Pupils will have to work in pairs or small groups in order that talking is seen by them to be part of the activity. They need to do something which requires some decision-making in order that several pupils debate the mathematics to come to some decisions. One task, often found in textbooks, asks pupils to sort triangles or other shapes according to a flow chart. So we will ask the pupils to create the flow chart to sort the triangle cards. Creating the flow chart requires decisions to be made, so this type of task would fit our needs (Figure 8.1).

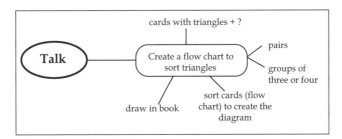

Figure 8.1 Talk as a focus

Pupils could be asked to draw the chart in their books, or we could provide them with cards which make up possible flow charts. The cards then have to be placed in some order, or rejected: 'Does the shape have one line of symmetry?' and 'Is the triangle isosceles?' may not both be necessary as decision boxes. The second form of the activity is more likely to provide opportunity for purposeful mathematical talk, because various alternatives are available for comparison and decision-making. Drawing the diagram in the book can become a 'first to finish activity' without much discussion. The transient nature of a diagram made using cards can also make it more easily alterable, and therefore worth checking. The original set of resource cards can be used to check the flow chart. The choice between the two approaches to the task lies with the teacher, but if talk is the major focus the decision is more likely to be for using the cards. You might challenge the pupils further by asking them to create a flow chart with the minimum number of cards to sort the triangles.

Write/read

If you want the lesson to focus on writing as an integral part of the task, the resource cards could be used for pupils to write descriptions of the cards, including all the properties they can identify (Figure 8.2).

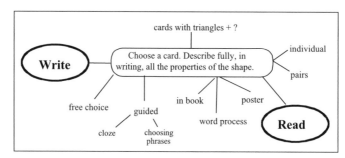

Figure 8.2 Write/read as a focus

Allowing individuals or pairs to work on the shapes on the cards without prompts may be a good way of assessing how much they can identify and how much they know about properties of triangles. With other pupils you may wish to provide descriptions and ask them to add the missing details (cloze) or offer phrases to be used. This may enable pupils to extend their vocabulary and help them to notice more about the shapes than they would with completely free choice. The choice of output could be as varied as writing in their own books, using a word processor or display work such as a poster.

You could combine this activity with a read activity. Pupils could swap descriptions and then match the pairs reading the descriptions to decide upon a match.

Move

Some children learn well when moving around; for others movement offers a hook to interest them in the mathematics of the task. Using movement as the other focus for the activity, the resource cards become something to sort (Figure 8.3). Each pupil has one card and they move themselves into groups where their cards have something in common. This movement could be instigated by the pupils or directed by the teacher.

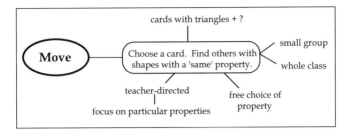

Figure 8.3 Move as a focus

This task might be used as a short activity, where the instruction is 'Get into groups of three, where your shapes have something in common'. Pupils then have to compare each other's cards and make their decisions based on any property. (Or this idea could be repeated over a longer session.) Alternatively, the teacher could choreograph the movement with a series of directions (probably requesting quiet, no conferring, as the pupils make their decisions).

- 'Those with at least one line of symmetry here, others over there.'
- 'If your shape has a right angle move here, otherwise move over there.'
- 'Decide whether your triangle has obtuse angles, acute angles or right angles. Form three groups.'
- 'Those with a right-angled triangle in this corner, those with an isosceles triangle in this corner, equilateral triangles over there and obtuse-angled triangles in that corner.'

The instructions can include conflict in the decision-making, as in the last case. Where does the isosceles right-angled triangle belong? Could you have an equilateral triangle in the isosceles corner?

These two types of lessons have much in common – the task, the resource and the movement – but the overall lesson style is very different. One offers lots of work on choice and comparing properties of shapes (especially if the pupils are expected to get in different groups of three), but although the pupils may talk a lot of mathematics but they may not be doing the mathematics you expect. The second version is tightly controlled by the teacher and allows for practice in response to the directions given. Each pupil, if they do not confer, is working on the properties of one shape.

Listen

Our pupils often see no purpose to listening; they can always ask the teacher for more help. Working actively on listening skills helps to encourage them to listen as well as providing an alternative approach to working on the content. Working on listening means that the pupils have to consider all the data before they begin the task (Figure 8.4).

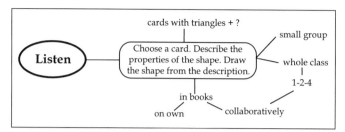

Figure 8.4 Listen as a focus

The teacher chooses a resource card and describes the properties of the shape, slowly and carefully. The pupils have to draw the shape. In pairs they compare their shapes, noting the properties the shapes have in common. The pairs compare this list with another pair, before the groups report their findings. A pupil could be the one to describe the shapes and your set of cards could have the properties on the back. This could then change into a group activity, rather than a whole-class activity. In terms of designing a lesson, you could do this for a few minutes, or for a whole lesson. The teacher needs to choose the appropriate style for the activity.

Imagine

Imagining has been part of a teacher's tool box for some years. It is very useful for exploring children's thinking and for analysing alternative conceptions and errors. Everyone can contribute because anything that is imagined has to be correct (this is always a good excuse for different ideas popping in) and each of the imaginings can contribute to the discussion. The activity needs to be adapted to allow some freedom for the imagination (Figure 8.5).

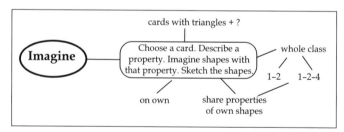

Figure 8.5 Imagine as a focus

The teacher chooses a resource card – an isosceles triangle, say – and selects one property. They may say, 'Imagine a bright red triangle, make it bigger, make it smaller, change it so that it has one line of symmetry. Fix it and tuck it in a corner. Now imagine a blue triangle with one line of symmetry, but different from the red one. Line them up. Which is bigger? Which parts are bigger? Is the perimeter bigger? Is the area bigger?' No answers are expected: these are questions for the pupils to make sure they look closely at their imaginary triangles. Ask them to sketch their triangles. Now offer another attribute –an obtuse angle, say. Do they need to change their triangles? If so get them to change them in their heads and think about some questions. Then get them to sketch their diagrams and compare the first and second sets. Get them to compare them with someone else's. You can then work on the different images with the whole class and talk about the properties of the diagrams and how they compare with the card chosen.

A second topic

Much of what has been described so far is based on experiences and tasks that we have found and adapted in the ways described earlier and used in classrooms. Let's try a different topic combined with a different resource. You need not limit yourself by the resource but it can sometimes allow you to extend your thinking in unexpected ways. The topic is area of rectangles; the resource we challenge ourselves with is a spreadsheet. This may lead to some strange ideas but they could be useful.

Talk

OK, so we cheated. The first idea is one we have used before, so in setting up the challenge we knew we could find an activity (Figure 8.6). (You could do this with Omnigraph for Windows, but we think the template focuses on the coordinates in a different way.)

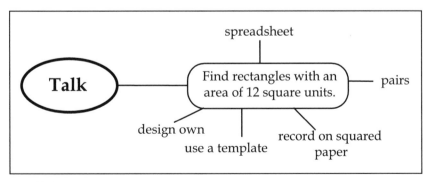

Figure 8.6 Talk

The task is not complicated, but the template might be. Scatter diagrams allow the spreadsheet to be used for plotting coordinates. A method of finding area, attributed to Descartes, allows area to be found for any coordinates:

> If you have four points which determine the shape, (x_1, y_1), (x_2, y_2), (x_3, y_3) and (x_4, y_4),
>
> area $= \frac{1}{2}[(x_1y_2 + x_2y_3 + x_3y_4 + x_4y_1) - (y_1x_2 + y_2x_3 + y_3x_4 + y_4x_1)]$

Pupils could design their own templates. If they keep the sides of the rectangle parallel to the axes, you may not need to give them Descartes's method! You could use Pythagoras's theorem for rectangles whose sides are not parallel to the axes. We are already moving on to the next aspect.

Write

If pupils design their own spreadsheet (Figure 8.7), they can be asked to write a report on how they did it and how they made decisions. This is even more interesting if pairs design the sheet.

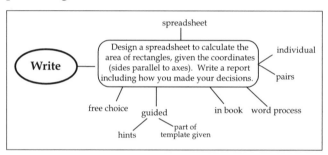

Figure 8.7 Write

Move

There is an obvious difficulty with this aspect – if you are working in a network room, there is no space to move. Perhaps this is better in a classroom with one computer, where the spreadsheet generates some data for us. Spreadsheets have formulas for generating random numbers, so we could write formulas for generating the sizes of the length and width of a rectangle (within our chosen limits).

We next need to think up what we can do with this. Suppose each pupil is given a rectangle (that way they can be all different). They could then move to one corner if the area of their rectangle is bigger than the one generated by the spreadsheet and to another if it is smaller, or stay put (Figure 8.8). You could imagine having other moves which depend on having the same or different lengths or widths, or having the same factor, and so on. Pupils then could try to decide what rectangles others have from the moves they make.

Does this seem too contrived? We don't know, we have never tried this. We have generated random numbers and used them in class but not for this activity.

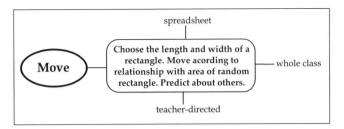

Figure 8.8 Move

Listen

There is a similar problem with a listening activity – perhaps the same form of spreadsheet could be used, but the class cannot see it (Figure 8.9). Clues are given to the area of the rectangle, such as 'it is 2 units longer than it is wide', 'its area is a multiple of 4' and so on. Pupils try to work out the area and dimensions of the rectangle.

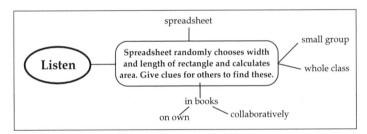

Figure 8.9 Listen

Imagine

Here is an idea we have used. This was suggested by some of our students in response to seeing some spreadsheet ideas (Figure 8.10). A template is designed to randomly choose the coordinates of the top right-hand corner of a rectangle. The opposite corner is at (0, 0) and the sides are parallel to the axes.

The class can choose the coordinates for the top right-hand corner of their rectangle. The template then calculates the difference in area between the two rectangles, as an area to the right and above (you need to decide how to show the area to the left and below). In Figure 8.11 the computer might have chosen (10, 7) and the class (4, 5). The area to the right would be given as 42 (6 × 7) and the area above as 20 (10 × 2). The pupils have to imagine the two rectangles to work out the relationship to try to find the coordinates that the spreadsheet has chosen.

Of course, you could work on these ideas with flash cards. You do not need the spreadsheet to do this for you; it is just easier once you have worked out how to do it.

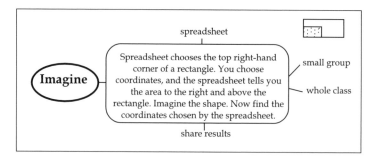

Figure 8.10 Imagine

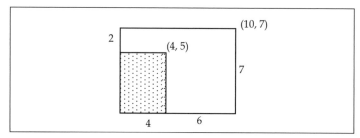

Figure 8.11 Imagining rectangles

The generality

Now it's time to try and work out the elements that make the different lessons. Looking back at the two sets of examples these are the things we would be looking for in the different lessons.

- *Talk*   Pupils need something to agree on/disagree with; come to agreement; tell others; share resources. Do something which requires some decision-making. Several pupils could debate the mathematics to come to some decisions.
- *Write*   Writing needs to be purposeful (writing answers that the teacher already knows, that are already in the back of the book is not a good selling point for all pupils). Something should happen to the writing (other than being assessed) during the lesson.
- *Move*   It makes a change to do an activity in which the pupils are allowed to move. Pupils could represent something that needs to be sorted, ordered or grouped.
- *Listen*   Get pupils to take full responsibility to listen to you. Pupils should have to do something with what they are hearing. Working on listening means that the pupils have to consider all the data before they begin the task.
- *Imagine*   This involves working with pupils to take their own ideas seriously. Images need to be shared in an atmosphere of trust and mutual respect.

Everyone's contribution needs to be valued so that different mathematical conceptions can be worked on.

• *Read* A crucial part of any test is reading, sifting information and making sense of it.

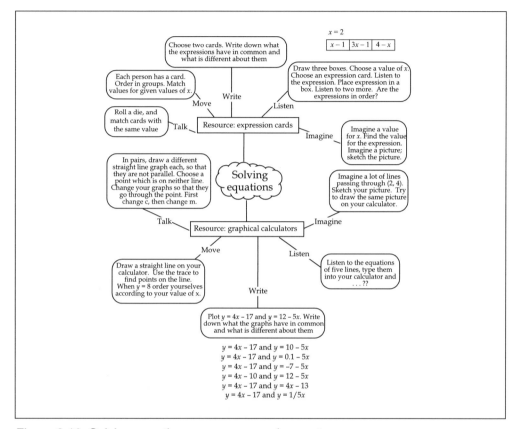

Figure 8.12 Solving equations: resources and aspects

Restricting ourselves to just one resource and expecting to find activities for all six aspects may be over ambitious, but the challenge remains. Figure 8.12 shows ideas using two different resources for solving equations.

Conclusion

There are many ways in which tasks can be adapted to suit these types of learner activities. A task which focuses on talk will feel very different for the learner than one which focuses on writing, or one which focuses on both. Using such aspects can provide the different experiences learners need as well as variety, which enhances the learning environment.

CHAPTER 9

Context, reality and ambiguity

In which we meet a bear and discuss the difference between problems that might be defined as real-life, realistic or relevant and learn to make the most of the ambiguities

In Chapter 8 we looked at aspects that learners bring to the lesson, but clearly only a selection of them. Two important facets which are missing are how the learners interpret what they are doing and how they work on problem solving; developing a curiosity about mathematics and a willingness to pose new questions.

Problem solving is a major aspect of the National Curriculum and the National Numeracy Strategy (NNS). In the National Curriculum, Ma1 is integrated through the rest of the curriculum with its key strands of problem solving, communicating and reasoning. In the NNS for Year 7, 'solving problems' is one of the six main strands. But what is problem solving? Are the problems real, are they realistic are they relevant and if so to whom and for what? In the NNS many of the suggestions for problems are word problems; they are closed, tightly defined and, you might say, unproblematic (DfEE 2000: draft section 2, pp. 30–38). For example, 'A map has a scale of 1cm to 6 km. A road measured on the map is 6.6cm long. What is the length of the road in kilometres?' (DfEE 2000: draft section 2, p. 31). There are few decisions to be made although the context is realistic, but there is little opportunity for Ma1.

What about the problems found in Standard Assessment Tasks (SATs) and GCSE papers? These are rich in questions which give rise to apocryphal stories, like that of the following GCSE probability question:

> Janet and John went camping and took tins of ham, beans and soup – three of each. For supper, having set up camp, they ate a tin of soup and a tin of ham. In the night there was a tremendous rainstorm and all the labels came off the remaining tins. What was the probability that the first tin that they opened in the morning contained beans?

Ignore all human curiosity raised by this question and ask no questions about Janet and John and their camping trip – the examination required 3/7 as an answer. The context may be 'real' but the mathematics problem is hardly relevant to anyone other than the question setter. However, a solution to the real problem was given by the candidate who offered the strategy of shaking the tins: 'Shake each of the tins. Each makes a different noise: the soup fairly sloppy, the beans less so and the ham not at all. The probability of opening beans is 1'. I hope that this solution got the candidate full marks.

Teacher advice for passing examination questions such as this would be to not treat the question as a real problem, but to ignore the context and look for the school mathematics. Children learn that lots of school mathematics problems are set in ridiculous contexts that are best ignored. Real-life problems allow for conversation and a more collegiate approach than is available in a timed written test. You might imagine Janet and John waking up and having a chat about the alternatives, or eating whatever is opened, or finding a cafe for breakfast since everything was soaked! Unfortunately part of the responsibility of the mathematics teacher is to help children answer examination questions regardless of poor attempts at contexts.

There are, however, lots of questions rich in possibilities due to the ambiguities arising from the context of the questions. By exploiting the ambiguities and working with the questions in different ways new classroom approaches emerge for learning mathematics. Without doubt there is also the possibility of creating a lot of garbage, so having played with the question whatever emerges needs to be analysed for its mathematical opportunities. There are a number of reasons for working in this way.

- Getting pupils to make ambiguities explicit may help us to work on their misconceptions.
- Ambiguities can be used to explore definitions and help in learning.
- Using the ambiguity forces us to look at explanations for answers, not just the answers themselves.
- Working with a context to unpick the reality can help the teacher to understand where the pupil is focused (often on a seemingly trivial aspect of context so that the mathematics is ignored).
- Working on the reality of the context can develop problem posing skills – learning to select the many variables which emerge as a result is an important aspect of problem solving.

To put you in the picture further, here is part of a reading that we have used with our ITE students. It is about mathematics questions in a television quiz show and the questions are being answered by a well-known bear:

'For fifty pounds here is question number two, and it's a two part question. Listen carefully.'

'If,' he said, 'you had a piece of wood eight feet long and you cut it in half, and if you cut the two pieces you then have into half, and if you then cut all the pieces into half again how many pieces would you have?'

'Eight' said Paddington promptly. 'Very good, bear,' said Ronnie Playfair approvingly . . .

'Here is the second part of the question. How long will each of the pieces be?'

'Eight feet' said Paddington, almost before the Master of Ceremonies had time to start the clock.

'Eight feet?' repeated Ronnie Playfair. 'You're sure you won't change your mind?'

'No, thank you, Mr Playfair,' said Paddington firmly.

'In that case . . . I must ask for the £5 back, the answer is one foot' . . .

'Oh, no, Mr Playfair' said Paddington politely. 'I'm sure that's right for your piece of wood but I cut mine the other way.'

'But if you're asked to cut a plank of wood in half,' stuttered Ronnie Playfair, 'you cut it across the middle not down the middle. It stands to reason.'

'Not if you're a bear' said Paddington, remembering his efforts at carpentry in the past. 'If you're a bear it's safer to cut it down the middle.'   (Bond 1971)

Paddington had already replied 'Two and a half' to the first question, 'How many buns make five?' (Paddington always shared his buns with Mr Gruber.) With 'No time at all' as the answer to the final question on filling a bath, Paddington went on to win the jackpot. His logic was impeccable and his explanations clear. (The bath had already been filled and he had been asked how long it would take to fill the same bath, with no mention of the bath having been emptied.) His challenge to us is 'What makes a good answer?' (and a good explanation). Alongside this is 'What makes a good question?' A discussion ensued with the students about these points and how as a teacher it is important to try and understand the logic in solutions given by pupils which at first glance seem incorrect. Allowing pupils to offer explanation of their solutions often gives a rich insight into their thinking.

During the quiz, Paddington uses a mixture of approaches to solving the problems: the idiosyncratic, the literal and the interpretative.

- *Idiosyncratic* In answering the buns question, Paddington's answer is completely idiosyncratic, depending on Paddington's own reality. The answer is logical in Paddington's terms but incomprehensible to others without the explanation.
- *Literal* In filling the bath, Paddington stays with the reality. His answer is totally literal. Realising that the 'same' bath needed no more filling shows how clear the reality is. Paddington understands the situation and can solve the real problem.
- *Interpretative* In cutting the wood the other way, Paddington offers us another interpretation. There is some ambiguity in the question, so there are other responses.

The first two types of responses help to make sense of misconceptions. The wood question offers a way of thinking which leads to new tasks.

Of course you need to beware of asking children to work with reality.

'You have seven sweeties in one hand and nine sweeties in your other hand. How many sweeties have you got altogether?'
'None' said Anna. 'I ain't got none in this hand and I ain't got none in this hand and so it's wrong to say I have if I ain't.'
Brave, brave Miss Haynes. 'I mean pretend, dear. Pretend that you have.'
Being so instructed Anna pretended and came out with the triumphant answer 'Fourteen.'
'Oh no, dear' said brave Miss Haynes. 'You've got sixteen. You see seven and nine makes sixteen.'
'I know that,' said Anna, 'but you said pretend, so I pretended to eat one and I pretended to give one away, so I've got fourteen.'   (Fynn 1974)

For Anna, her reality is stronger than the traditional mathematics answer that was expected. An answer without an explanation would lead to Anna getting her work marked with a cross, yet she knows the mathematics; she is going with the implied reality in her own way.

In what follows we present our ideas for creating ideas for the classroom by considering the context within given questions, by exploiting any ambiguities and using different approaches for pupils to learn mathematics. We have broken down the sequence of events for you to follow as:

- Job 1: restoring the reality, identifying the variables.
- Job 2: playing with the mathematics.
- Job 3: handling the variables/imposing some constraints.
- Job 4: defining some tasks.

The first group of questions is set in a 'real' context and we will use this routine to adapt them into new tasks. The second group of questions is set within a mathematical context but we will use the same framework to develop the mathematics and the teaching approaches.

A textbook question: strips of paper

Here is one of twenty textbook questions from an exercise on division:

How many 7cm lengths can be cut from a paper strip which is 161cm long?
(School Mathematics Project (SMP) 1985: 16)

At first glance it may seem quite straightforward but it actually offers many different possibilities. The solutions can still be found by division and checked by multiplying but the different interpretations offer a richer mathematical task to the pupils. The questions open up if you restore the reality – if you start asking questions about the real context of the problem.

Job 1: restoring the reality, identifying the variables

Close your eyes and visualise the strip. Imagine cutting it. Now (remember Paddington) how wide is the long strip you are cutting? How wide is your strip? Which way will you make the cut? Responding to each of the questions leads to a variety of options:

- If the long strip is 7cm wide I can cut 161 strips of width 1cm, or 332 of width 0.5cm, and so on.
- If the strip is 14cm wide . . .
- If the 7cm strip has to be 1cm wide and the long strip is 2cm wide I can calculate 161 × 2 ÷ 7, and so on.
- If the 7cm has to be cut on the diagonal I might need to think about the hypotenuse of a right-angled triangle . . .
- If I fold and cut . . .

Suddenly, from what seems to be a fairly mundane textbook question, there is a wealth of possibilities for other classroom activities that still involve division. Some decision-making, communication and explanation are required in each of the listed alternatives, but the processes of mathematics are inextricably mixed with the arithmetic. A problem is emerging which requires solution and justification. Ma1 can be seen to be permeating Ma2, as required by the National Curriculum.

Job 2: playing with the mathematics

For most of you the questions can be answered easily (not so the pupils). If not, explore them. Can you come up with some general results? We need to consider the mathematics in the task at our own level first. The task which is likely to challenge at our level is the question which involves cutting across a diagonal. The mathematics now moves into the use of the Pythagoras's theorem (Figure 9.1).

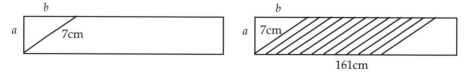

Figure 9.1 Cutting paper strips – consider the hypotenuse question, where the strip is cut on bias

First explain how the strips can be parallel and equal. If each strip is $n\,cm$ wide then the number of strips would be $\frac{161-b}{n}$ where $b = \sqrt{49 - a^2}$. How do the answers vary for different values of a? What area of paper is wasted?

Job 3: handling the variables/imposing some constraints

The decision now lies with the teacher which task or how many of the tasks to use. What mathematics do you wish to focus on? Do you wish to consider different representations of area and how these relate to multiplication? The task involving different strips $7 \times n$ cut from a $161 \times p$ strip may be begun by giving the value of p and a set of values for n, with pupils finding special cases before choosing the values for themselves, or by brainstorming with the class possible values and their implications before they test them for themselves. The ultimate intention may or may not be to arrive at a generalised formula.

Choosing to exploit the task to practise the use of Pythagoras's theorem may need the variables limiting differently for different classes. A bright Year 11 class might be expected to decide for themselves, but for another class you might choose a and thus fix b and/or you might fix n to be 1 or any other convenient or inconvenient number.

Job 4: defining some tasks

The tasks now need to be written in a form to use so that they are mathematically valid, reasonable and interesting with some purpose other than getting one right answer.

How many 7cm × 1cm strips can be cut from a paper strip which is 161cm long and 2cm wide?
What if the long strip was 3cm (4cm, 10cm, 20cm, 100cm and so on) wide?

How many 7cm × 1cm strips can be cut from a paper strip which is 161cm long and 5cm wide?
What if the strips to be cut were 0.5cm (0.4cm, 1.25cm, 2.5cm and so on) wide?

How many 7cm × 1cm strips can be cut from a paper strip which is 161cm long and 7cm wide?
What if the strips to be cut were 0.5cm (23cm, 3.5cm, 11.5cm and so on) wide?

> How many 7cm × 1cm strips can be cut from a paper strip which is 161cm long
> if the 7cm has to be cut on the diagonal?
> Suppose the 161cm strip is 3cm wide. Suppose it is 1cm (2cm and so
> on) wide?

An NNS problem: a piece of wood

We couldn't resist including this question, as it is so like the Paddington question.

> A plank of wood weighs 1.4kg. I cut off 25cm. The plank now weighs 0.8kg. What
> was the length of the original plank?   (DfEE 2000: draft section 2, p. 31)

The writers are assuming no ambiguity. It has similarities with the previous
question, but analysis can take us into different areas of mathematics.

Job 1: restoring the reality, identifying the variables

As before, imagine the piece of wood and imagine cutting it. What is the overall
shape of the piece of wood? What is its width and length? Does thickness matter?
Why do you think 25cm is being cut from the wood? Which way can your wood
be cut? Can it be cut across the width, along the length, across a diagonal? Why
have the masses been given? In how many different ways can 25cm be cut off so
that 0.6kg is removed from the plank?

Figure 9.2 shows various ways that the wood might be cut with the shaded part
representing 0.6kg of the plank and the remaining part representing 0.8kg of the
plank. As yet we have not analysed the mathematical possibilities; that is to come!

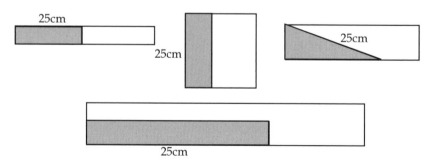

Figure 9.2 Ways of cutting wood

Job 2: playing with the mathematics

The mathematics of ratio is not as clear as the rectangles in the previous task, so first we need to question some of our own knowledge.

The plank in Figure 9.3 has to be divided in the ratio 3:4 (the masses are 0.6:0.8, giving a total of 1.4kg) so 25cm is $\frac{3}{7}$ of the overall length of the plank. How do we know that the width of the plank is unnecessary to the solution? Would it be better to give the pupils a variety of widths to discover this?

If the plank is 25cm wide, is the length a variable (Figure 9.4)? If there is only one solution, what other data do we need to collect?

25cm

0.6kg	0.8kg

Figure 9.3 Plank 1

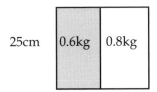

25cm

Figure 9.4 Plank 2

Suppose the cut is diagonal (Figure 9.5). Do *x* and *y* have to be in a certain proportion before the division into $\frac{3}{7} : \frac{4}{7}$ is possible? Is such a division possible?

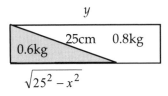

Figure 9.5 Plank 3

In Figure 9.6, if the width (say *a*) of the new piece of wood is different from the width of the plank, for what values of *x* and *y* is there a solution?

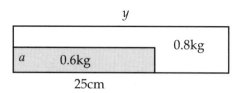

Figure 9.6 Plank 4

Job 3: handling the variables/imposing some constraints

If 25cm is cut off the width or the length of a given piece of wood, then the proportions of the two pieces may be different. A first idea is to fix the size of the piece of wood and explore the two aspects (Figure 9.7).

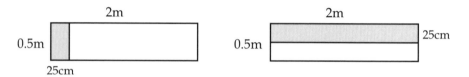

Figure 9.7 Cutting a piece of wood in two ways

If the piece of wood is 0.5m × 2m, cutting 25cm off the length gives two pieces in the ratio 1:7, whereas cutting 25cm off the width gives two pieces in the ratio 1:1. Pupils could be asked to find different lengths and widths of pieces of wood and the appropriate ratios. When do you get the same ratios? Why? For what dimensions of plank do you get the ratio 3:7 (Figure 9.8)? Can pupils move towards the generalisation that the length is the major aspect when the 25cm is cut off the width? Are they likely to choose non-integer dimensions?

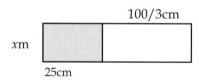

Figure 9.8 A generalisation

If we want pupils to work on the ratio, would it be better to choose a ratio such as 5:7, as in the context of wood dimensions as infinite decimals are unrealistic?

Now the task being generated is about trying out ideas to do with proportion with the context suggesting mathematical practice on ratio.

Job 4: defining some tasks

A piece of wood measures 0.5m × 2m. When 25cm is chopped off (try taking the piece off both length and width) it weighs 0.5kg. What does the remaining piece weigh?
Try this for other sizes of the piece of wood.

What dimensions might a piece of wood be if, when a 25cm piece weighing 0.5kg is chopped off, the remaining piece(s) weighs 0.7kg?

What dimensions might a piece of wood be if, when a 25cm piece weighing 0.6kg is chopped off, the remaining piece(s) weighs 0.8kg?

Suppose a plank weighs 1.4kg and measures 0.5m × 1m. Is it possible to cut a 25cm length so that it weighs 0.6kg?

Another NNS problem: coffee beans

Here is another problem taken from the 'numbers and the number system' section of the NNS, and offered as an example of a 'simple' question.

Coffee is made from two types of beans, from Java and Columbia in the ratio 2:3. How much of each type of bean will be needed to make 500 grams of coffee?
(DfEE 2000: draft section 2, p. 17)

Job 1: restoring the reality, identifying the variables

'I don't want coffee in that ratio, I prefer . . ..' Imagine buying the coffee. What if you prefer more (less) Columbian beans in the mixture? Do you mind whether you get exactly 500g? Do you prefer to buy the coffee by cost? How does the coffee get measured? Is it served using scoops or by weight? Would a mix of three different beans be more enjoyable?

Job 2: playing with the mathematics

Why has the person who wrote the question chosen the ratio 2:3 and the total quantity of coffee as 500g? As teachers we know that the ratio implies five equal shares and 500 is a multiple of 5. This is the key mathematical aspect of ratio in this question. This is the mathematics we would like our pupils to know.

Suppose the ratio was not 2:3. What other numbers would we choose? We might choose 1:4, 7:3 or 21:29 because they sum to 5, 10 and 50, respectively, and 500 is a multiple of all of these numbers. Why not 3:4 or 1:8? Well, 7 and 9 are not factors of 500. We might use these ratios if we are not concerned about the final weight of the coffee: three scoops to four scoops is just as easy as one scoop to four scoops, but $214\frac{2}{7}$ g and $285\frac{5}{7}$ g are rather more complex. How might we set up a task that allows us to explore the relationship between the weight and the parts of the ratio?

If I were interested in cost, would I prefer to buy £5 worth of coffee? How does this affect the ratio?

Job 3: handling the variables/imposing some constraints

If we stay with 500g of coffee and two types of beans, we could work from the weight to possible ratios and identify the ratios from there, which might lead us to recognise the connection. For example, 100g of Javan beans and 400g of Columbian beans would be in the ratio 1:4; 150g and 350g would be in the ratio 3:7, and so on. This might give too many solutions, too many special cases, which might distract from the generalisation. We could assume that the beans are served in automatic scoops of 50g to limit the number of options; this would give us 50g and 450g, or 1:9, say. This may be too limiting, so we could use 25g (or 20g) or three (or more) types of beans and look at the ratios. So 100g of Javan beans, 200g of Columbian beans and 200g of Kenyan beans gives a ratio of 1:2:2, or 150g, 250g and 100g would have the ratio 3:5:2.

Cost is a variable which is often very important in real shopping. Do different beans cost different prices? Could we extend the task to include prices? Does the mathematics change if I fix the cost? In real life extracting data about cost usually means reading from the list with more information than we need.

Job 4: defining some tasks

> Coffee made from a mixture of two types of beans, from Java and Columbia, is sold. If I buy 500g of coffee, how much of each type of bean could this be? Write the ratio in its simplest form. What do the ratios have in common?

Coffee made from a mixture of two, three or four types of beans, Javan, Columbian, Kenyan and Continental roast, is sold. The coffee is delivered from its store barrel in 25g scoops. If I buy 500g of coffee, how much of each type of bean is this? Write the ratio in its simplest form. What do the ratios have in common?

The last version might be explored using a spreadsheet:

Coffee made from a mix of two, three or four types of beans, Javan, Columbian, Kenyan and Continental roast, is sold. The coffee is delivered from its store barrel in 25g scoops. If I buy 500g of coffee, how much of each type of bean is this?

How much will the coffee cost?

Beans	Price per 100g
House roast	£0.83
Continental roast	£1.04
Columbia	£0.92
Java	£1.14
Kenya	£1.13

Can I spend exactly £7, if I can choose any mix of coffee?

Ways of using the tasks

As teachers, we may begin to see different uses for these types of task, depending on the mathematics we want to work with and the stage at which our pupils are meeting them. The coffee bean problem starts to become something which could act as an introductory task, to develop the mathematics of ratio and proportion from an understanding of the context. The strip of paper problem is more likely to be used for practising how to set up multiplication and division problems extracted from the context or for offering a context in which to practise Pythagoras's theorem.

A GCSE problem: exchanging money

Here is a fairly typical context laden question from a GCSE paper:

When Alison went to Austria the exchange rate was 16 Austrian Schillings for each £1. Alison changed £384. Calculate how many Austrian Schillings she received.
Northern Examination and Assessment Board, Paper 2, Tier I, June 1997, Qu. 8

This is different from the previous tasks in that any new questions which emerge are related to what might be a real solution of the problem.

Job 1: restoring the reality, identifying the variables

If you have ever exchanged money, you know that this is unlikely to be the question that you would ask. It fails to consider the commission charged for changing the money. Is it charged to a credit card? Is there an extra commission for this? If you are shopping for holiday money, you will want to know more than just the exchange rate. The question really wants you to calculate 384 × 16, but if you stay with the context you will want to do more than this. I may have a rough idea of how much I want, say £400. The agent is unlikely to offer me coins, unless I am actually in Austria, in which case the agent will not want the £4 in £1 coins. So where am I exchanging the money? If I am in Austria, am I changing travellers' cheques? If that is the case I would not pay commission at this stage, but I am unlikely to have cheques in strange amounts like £4, nor would I change so much at once. So what questions would I ask?

Job 2: playing with the mathematics

The reality of the situation demands some awareness of exchange rates. Should we survey various travel agents? Could we look on the internet? What are the rates of commission? Do I want to be able to change money back at the end of my holiday? Are there any deals for this? If I want to buy travellers' cheques do I want sterling, euros or dollars? What happens to the exchange rate now? What is the commission? Do I want to change all my money in one go, or will I change some as I go? The problem is now one of data handling: what data must be collected to optimise the solution. Do I want the easiest task – the local agent? Do I want the most schillings? The posing of questions at this stage is in order to identify the variables in the problem in order to look for methods of solution; finding the mathematics depends on what route to the solution you want. The task only has purpose if the reality is restored to the mathematics.

Job 3: handling the variables/imposing some constraint

If this task is set up for pupils in the original form above, the task can provide an opportunity for them to control the variables in deciding the 'best' solution to the task. It is then the pupils' choice to impose the constraints.

Suppose the problem is based on exchanging all the money in the UK before leaving. The task is then to find the rates at different agents or banks for approximately £400 and working on different amounts of schillings (rounded to suit 100 schilling notes) with the relevant commission.

The problem could be compared with buying travellers' cheques and changing them over a time when the exchange rate is likely to vary.

Perhaps the best solution is the quickest. What do I get from the first place I visit?

Job 4: defining some tasks

Here we offer a couple of versions which account for the reality more firmly. As a teacher you may wish the pupils to come up with these versions of the task. Developing such questions is a major part of the PCAI process described in Chapter 2. It also provides a way of helping our learners to develop problem solving skills.

> Find the exchange rate for converting to Austrian schillings from pounds sterling and the commission charges for exchanging money from at least three agents or banks. Work out how many schillings you would obtain for approximately £400.

> Find the cost of buying travellers' cheques to the value of £400 from at least three agents or banks. Find the exchange rate of Austrian schillings with pounds sterling from the internet every day for two weeks. Imagine changing your money on three of those days. Work out how many schillings you would obtain. What is the real exchange rate you obtained?

Plotting coordinates

> Plot the coordinates (4, 5), (4, 1) and (6, 3). Which letter of the alphabet is this?

This is not what anyone would call a context question – it is only ever seen in mathematics classrooms. The reason for including this is to consider the ways we might use the learners' own understandings of coordinates to make the conventions more memorable.

Job 1: restoring the reality, identifying the variables

The reality of plotting coordinates is the fact that it is a convention, and not an infallible truth. There is nothing wrong in other interpretations, but we adopt a convention so that others will understand; so that we share a language. As teachers we are used to children failing to remember the order in which to plot coordinates. We use different ways of helping our pupils to remember: 'x is first in the alphabet do that first'; 'x is a cross, so go across first'; and so on. Although it is a convention, which we spend a lot of time practising, there is no valid reason why it should be. Perhaps we should spend more time on the alternatives.

Job 2: playing with the mathematics

Some things have to be part of the system: somewhere to start and two 'directions'. The rest is free choice. Dave Hewitt (1999) calls these two aspects 'necessary and arbitrary'. In Figure 9.9 the first diagram shows a perfectly good interpretation of (4, 5). The axes do not show x or y, but most people would be able to follow the convention and plot (2, 5) or (4, 3), say. The axes in the second diagram are more difficult to use, but you could soon learn how to use the system.

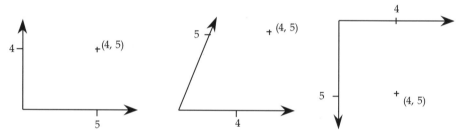

Figure 9.9 Different ways of plotting (4, 5)

The third example is just as easy to follow as the conventional system. Why do we not use that? Is there some connection to other aspects of mathematics, which make us follow particular rules? Who was Descartes? Why is his choice the one we follow?

We have not mentioned polar coordinates. The two numbers in polar coordinates refer to different units of measure: length and angle. Could we think of any other units of measure?

Job 3: handling the variables/imposing some constraints

The variables are:

- the position of the origin;
- which axis to use first;
- the orientation of the axes relative to each other;
- length as the attribute of the two numbers in the coordinate pair.

Job 4: defining some tasks

> Plot the point (4, 5) in as many different ways as you can. Explain your conventions.

> In pairs, play 'Name me!' One of the pair chooses an origin and which way to plot the coordinates and plots a point for the other person to guess. The other guesses a coordinate pair and this is plotted by the first player according to the conventions chosen. This is repeated until the point is named correctly. Score by counting the number of tries.

The program MicroSMILE for Windows, 'Pack 5: Coordinates', includes an activity called Locate, where players are asked to identify coordinates when they do not know the conventions.

> Bart Simpson says, 'I am cleverer than Descartes! You don't need a coordinate pair, just give me one number to plot the point. If you say 25 I will plot (5, 5) in Cartesian coordinates. If you say 35, I will plot (7, 5)'. Try plotting 6, 12 or –24. What is wrong with Bart's system?

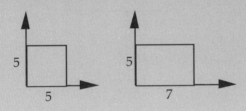

You could challenge your pupils to come up with their own systems.

This example shows that we can exploit the idea of ambiguity in more mathematical contexts (like how many nines in 171). Think of the problem pupils have with something like '2a'. Working on their interpretations, we believe, can help them to accept the definition of '2 multiplying some number represented by a', not 'two apples' or '20 a' and so on.

An investigation: egg boxes

> How many ways can you place two eggs in an egg box which holds half a dozen eggs?

This is not a 'real' question. The context serves as shorthand for the task. The problem we have found with this type of labelling is that pupils stay with the idea that they are doing 'egg boxes' and often miss the mathematics.

Job 1: restoring the reality, identifying the variables

What is this question really about? The eggs and the box are simply an image for placing two objects in a 2 × 3 array. Is it a 'real' box; one with a lid? Does this change the task? What if it is not a 2 × 3 array but a 1 × 6 array? Does the shape of the box change the answer?

  This task is very like the shading of $\frac{1}{3}$ in Chapter 6. It is not about different images for fractions (although you could make that link); it is about being systematic, working on combinations, justifying your decision to stop and accounting for the total number of solutions. Much of the work comes from Ma1 – hence the way the task tends to come with its label as an investigation – but it contains mathematical content as well as process. The task is about not egg boxes, but combinations.

Job 2: playing with the mathematics

This is a task where symmetry plays a large role in justifying solutions; placing 0 eggs is the same as placing 6, placing 1 is the same as placing 5 and placing 2 is the same as placing 4, so that the task has only four mathematical variations if you are changing the number of eggs.

  In placing two eggs, you have to decide whether or not to accept the symmetry of a 2 × 3 array, or to stay with the literal: the box has a lid so the array has a definite top and bottom. How do the answers differ? How do they relate to the answers we would obtain from a 1 × 6 array. Are the answers the same? When? Does this have anything to do with the formula $^{n}C_{r} = n!/r!(n-r)!$?

  If we assume the box has a lid, the answer for no eggs or six eggs is 1, for one egg or five eggs it is 6, and for two or four eggs it is 15. The sequence is 1, 6, 15 or 15, 6, 1. Where have you seen these numbers before? What does Pascal's triangle have to do with egg boxes?

Job 3: handling the variables/imposing some constraints

The variables are:

- the number of eggs;
- the size of the box;
- the arrangement of the individual cells;
- the shape and symmetry of the box.

Job 4: defining some tasks

The task can remain the same – the work on the task can be extended by the pupils into the mathematical areas above – especially if they are encouraged to use a touch of 'what-if-not'. Or you can make the intended extension more explicit in the wording of the task.

> How many ways can you place two eggs in an egg box which holds half a dozen eggs? How does your answer change for different numbers of eggs? What would happen if you changed the egg box?

You may expect your pupils to do these adaptations for themselves by making the question less defined.

> Investigate how many ways you can place eggs in an egg box.

The analysis which has happened here highlights the directions pupils might take and these ideas can be explored with them.

An investigation: frogs

> There are two teams of three frogs sitting on a line of seven lily pads, leaving one space between the teams. If frogs are allowed to slide on to an empty lily pad or hop over one frog on to an empty lily pad, how many moves does it take the teams to swap over?

There is obviously no reality in this question, the context is a way of using the language of jumps and hops. The problem is fascinating – you can buy lovely versions of this as a game – and it is this very fascination which can be the difficulty. It can be such fun to do that you forget to do the mathematics!

Job 1: restoring the reality, identifying the variables

The game is first about finding a solution, and that can be quite frustrating! The mathematics lies in the patterns which can be found in the solution and whether this can be extended to other numbers of frogs and lily pads. If this can be extended, is there a pattern to the solutions? Can the solutions be generalised? Can the generalisation be proved?

The variables are the number of frogs, the number of lily pads and the rules about hopping and sliding. If the number of frogs is increased, but the size of the teams stays the same as each other, the formula for predicting the number of moves is a quadratic. Can we draw the curve? Is it a parabola or just the dots?

Job 2: playing with the mathematics

Let's vary the number of frogs and keep one spare lily pad. It is much easier to begin with one frog on each side. Table 9.1 shows the moves if there is one (two, three, etc.) frog on each side, where S represents sliding and H represents hopping.

If we do the difference table (Table 9.2) for the total number of moves for the games with different numbers of frogs we find the second difference is a constant, 2, implying $n \rightarrow n^2 +$ something. But what?

Table 9.1 Frogs and moves

No. of frogs n	No. of lily pads (p)	Moves	Total
1	3	SHS	3
2	5	SHSHHSHS	8
3	7	SHSHHSHHHSHHSHS	15
4	9	SHSHHSHHHSHHHHSHHHSHHSHS	24
5	11	SHSHHSHHHSHHHHSHHHHHSHHHHSHHHSHHSHS	35

Table 9.2 Difference table

n	1		2		3		4		5
p	3		8		15		24		35
1st difference		5		7		9		11	
2nd difference			2		2		2		
Guess: n^2	1		4		9		16		25
$n^2 + 2n$	3		8		15		24		35

The pattern is also easily spotted as 1×3, 2×4, 3×5, etc. This allows a nice comparison of the different algebraic expressions: $n(n + 2)$ and $n^2 + 2n$.

The other pattern lies in the slides and hops (Table 9.3). Look back at Table 9.1 to see where the numbers in the second column come from.

Table 9.3 Analysing slides and hops

n	Slides and hops		
1	1 1 1	1 1 and 1	2 + 1
2	1 1 1 2 1 1 1	1 1 1 and 1 2 1	3 + 1 + 2 + 1
3	1 1 1 2 1 3 1 2 1 1 1	1 1 1 1 and 1 2 3 2 1	4 + 1 + 2 + 3 + 2 + 1
4	1 1 1 2 1 3 1 4 1 3 1 2 1 1 1	1 1 1 1 1 and 1 2 3 4 3 2 1	5 + 1 + 2 + 3 + 4 + 3 + 2 + 1

Why does the number pattern in the last column give the total $n^2 + 2n$?

Can we prove that these results will always work? What do we know about number sequences which will help?

Job 3: handling the variables/imposing some constraints

The variables are:

- the number of frogs;
- the number of lily pads;
- the rules about hopping and sliding;
- the arrangement of frogs at the start;
- the shape of the arrangement (does a circle make a difference?);
- the methods of recording.

You can begin to see the pull of 'what-if-not' again.

Job 4: defining some tasks

As with the egg boxes, the original task can lead you down many paths – if you are used to following them. There is no real need to change the task; just change the approach, remembering the mathematics.

Doing a Paddington

In operating with the type of logic Paddington shows in answering the quiz questions, we can begin to be more aware of the potential ambiguities in a question.

> A lorry will carry 5 tonnes. How many half tonne crates will fit on the lorry?

If you were Paddington approaching the lorry question, would you ask how big the crates are? Is the lorry already full? You could offer a variety of answers, but every answer needs to be accompanied by a reason. Even if you met this question in an examination, you ought to provide something like '10 crates is the maximum possible number, but they will only fit if the sizes of the crates suit the size of the lorry'.

The questions that this task prompts may seem irrelevant and a bit confusing for the classroom, but they are important questions if you are solving problems in real life. In the mathematics classroom, we rarely deal with real life, so our pupils are expected to ignore such things, but what if they cannot? What if they stay with the reality, like Paddington answering the bath question? What if they are in their own reality, like Anna? How do we work on these issues? Can we work on them and do a lot of mathematics at the same time? With such tasks, you can.

When you analyse questions like the GCSE paper 'exchanging money' question and think about Paddington's unorthodox approach, you begin to realise the interference reality can have on your thinking. Those of us who are good at mathematics know the rules of the game in examination questions. We know that we just have to extract the numbers and do a multiplication: the context is a clue to the operation, not a reality. If I stay interested in the reality of the context then £384 becomes a sum of money to be rejected with 'Well, I wouldn't change that much' or 'I'd change £400' as well as questions about commission and so on. As teachers we can exploit the reality to make the questions worth answering and at the same time help our pupils to understand what examination questions are demanding of them.

Our reasons for working on questions in this way are:

- to create questions where there is more than one answer, to extend the practice within the task;
- to use context to explore mathematical ideas using images which may help pupils to remember the mathematics;
- to help pupils pose questions in order to develop their skills in solving real-life problems – i.e. what data need to be collected and why;

- to help pupils to explore the reality of context questions because, we believe, by ignoring the detail we actually make it difficult for some children to appreciate the task because they stay with the context;
- to help pupils to explore the ambiguities in questions, to appreciate alternative ideas and use any confusion to work on the pupils' skills of explaining;
- because some contexts can make it easier for pupils to remember the mathematics.

Working on the coffee bean questions, offers an extended way of working on ratio and proportion. The connection between the sum of the parts of the ratio and our tendency to use multiples of this number for the amount to be shared can be explored in a context which constrains the number in a useful way. It also provides a useful place holder. If you have spent a few lessons working on the ratio of coffee beans, 'coffee beans' can act as a reminder to pupils of their ideas on ratio. It also means that there are lots of questions without having to write out a worksheet!

Ambiguity can also help creativity. Once you realise there are alternative ways of looking at such questions, you begin to look for them: 'How many nines in 171?' – '0, 19, 1 (1 + 7 + 1), or even 8 (1 + 71)'. Much more fun!

References

Bond, M. (1971) *Paddington at Large*. London: Collins.

Department for Education and Employment (DfEE) (2000) *The National Numeracy Strategy – Framework for Teaching Mathematics: Year 7*. Draft 3/00. London: DfEE. www.standards.dfee.gov.uk/numeracy/NNSframework (accessed 23 November 2000).

Fynn (1974) *Mister God, This is Anna*. London: William Collins.

Hewitt, D. (1999) 'Arbitrary and necessary, part 1: a way of viewing the mathematics curriculum', *For the Learning of Mathematics* 19(3), 2–9.

School Mathematics Project (1985) *SMP 11–16 Book B2*. Cambridge: Cambridge University Press.

CHAPTER 10

Connecting the syllabus

In which we meet a syllabus and use it to develop activities that involve different aspects of mathematics

Most teachers use schemes of work. There is an expectation in England and Wales that we will use the National Curriculum. Teachers are expected to account for whether their pupils have covered all the topics in the form expected by such syllabuses. Most mathematics teachers are accustomed to doing this: reading the scheme/syllabus; looking at what is expected in the examination/test; and then planning activities accordingly with or without a textbook. When planning with a syllabus, you will probably consider the mathematical progression through the topics as well as what needs repeated practice, what concepts are brand new, what aspects need to be rehearsed in advance of new work and what may be glimpsed for future exploration. You will decide how to:

- create activities to practise key skills in as wide a range of contexts as possible;
- organise the topics across the time period to integrate the different strands of mathematics;
- provide a variety of learning experiences.

In terms of wider planning we hope that you will have picked up one of our particular beliefs from this book, that different learners need different approaches. We also think that, having taught something, you then need to take every opportunity to re-present it. If variety is the spice of life, we need to consider as many different styles of activities as possible during the many years of the pupils' mathematical experiences.

What we will do in this chapter is take a chunk of a syllabus and explore ways to devise activities to connect across the range of topics. We will use all the ideas from the preceding chapters with the main new idea being the challenge to combine different topic areas.

A syllabus

The first place to start thinking about connecting across the curriculum is a scheme and where better than the National Numeracy Strategy (DfEE 2000)? Pupils in primary schools are used to it and the scheme is beginning to influence work in secondary schools, with a framework for Year 7 offered for September 2000.

The NNS offers a syllabus ('pupils should be taught to . . .') and exemplar questions ('as outcomes pupils should . . .') just like the current National Curriculum and just like the GCSE examination boards, which offer syllabuses and examination papers. There is no advice on how to move from the teaching aim to the learning outcome other than by inference. Progression through the mathematics needs to be determined by the teacher.

Table 10.1 shows the NNS syllabus for the second half of the autumn term in Year 7. It is called a medium-term plan but in fact is not a plan in the sense of planning for teaching. Like many schemes and textbooks, it is a list of topics to be covered (although some of the topics are also in the scheme given for other times of the year). We have chosen to work with this scheme, as it is apparently even more prescriptive than the many versions of the National Curriculum, in that it suggests the hours that the topic will be taught and seems to imply an order. The NNS (DfEE 2000) comes in three sections so references to it give the section number and page.

Table 10.1 NNS syllabus, Year 7, autumn term, part 2

Section	Hours	Pages	Topics
1	6	10–17	Fractions, decimals and percentages
		20–25	Mental methods
		18–19	Number operations
		29–38	Solving problems, checking results
2	6	39–43	Equations and formulas
		30–38	Solving problems
3	3	80–84	Probability
4	3	65	Coordinates
		56–59	Properties of shapes

(DfEE 2000: draft section 1, p. 30)

The six hours in the first row of the table indicates about two weeks of mathematics lessons on the topics in the first section. It also seems to indicate that mental methods are separate from fractions etc. and that both come before number operations. Fortunately reality reigns. The NNS states that the 'order is not sacrosanct, and can be changed to suit the pupils you teach and your own preferences' (draft section 1, p. 17) and that the teacher is left to 'develop day-to-day lessons based on your choice of activities and resources for your pupils' (draft section 1, p. 15). Anyway, spending two weeks on fractions, decimals and percentages at the beginning of the half term is unlikely to result in pupils remembering these topics by the end of the same term. Longer term retention of this content is even more unlikely, besides the fact that spending two weeks on these topics could be mind-numbingly boring!

As well as the number of hours and list of topics, a further dimension, key objectives, is prescribed in the NNS. Key objectives are defined as 'central to all pupils' achievement in relation to National Curriculum levels' (draft section 1, p. 3); they are a sort of super selection from the syllabus. For the second half of the autumn term these are:

- Use the equivalence of fractions, decimals and percentages in describing proportions
- Know and use order of operations
- . . . extend mental methods of calculation to include decimals, fractions and percentages
- Judge whether an answer is reasonable and check results, including using:
  - knowledge of the number system
  - rounding to approximate
  - inverse operations
- Choose and justify the use of an appropriate and efficient method for solving a problem
- Use letters or symbols to represent unknown numbers or variables
- Know that algebraic operations follow the same conventions and order as arithmetic operations
- . . . know that probabilities lie between 0 and 1, and calculate probabilities based on equally likely outcomes in simple contexts

(DfEE 2000: draft section 1, pp. 28–9)

Would you have chosen these to be your key objectives? You may want to change the priorities as you know your pupils. That's a different issue. We are going to work to this structure, as we are not thinking about a particular set of pupils. You will need to adapt all activities for the short- and long-term needs of the individuals you are helping to learn mathematics.

Is there a strategy for planning across a scheme of work? Yes, there are many! This book, however, is mainly about creating activities and so we will offer not so much a plan but ideas for connecting the curriculum within an activity using ideas from the previous chapters: not so much a plan but part of your planning, part of preparing for teaching. We set out to devise some activities with the NNS syllabus and the key objectives in mind, analysing and linking the topics, firstly within sections and then across them, using the key objectives as areas which need major focus and which will probably need revisiting in many contexts. Later in the chapter we will challenge ourselves to create activities connecting other aspects of mathematics, to offer you examples of different relationships.

Linking within sections

The NNS describes the content of the mathematics for the half term. The document also gives examples of the types of 'appropriate' questions that might be asked at this level, but as final assessment outcomes and not as practice for doing mathematics.

Let us consider section 1 and at the outset get rid of 'solving problems' as a focus for teaching. All mathematics offered to pupils is some kind of problem to be solved, requiring a solution to be found (see Chapter 8). Solving problems is not a topic to be taught. Similarly 'mental methods' is a permanent possible strategy for solution but not an area of mathematical content. This leaves us with fractions, decimals, percentages and number operations. Let us next choose an area for teaching. Suppose the decision is to teach about equivalent fractions.

Creating connections within section 1
Here are some typical suggestions for equivalent fraction work:

- Continue the pattern: $\frac{4}{5} = \frac{8}{10} = \frac{12}{15} = \frac{16}{20} =$
- Find the missing number: $\frac{4}{5} = \frac{?}{20}$
- Find the missing number: $\frac{4}{?} = \frac{20}{25}$

We have posed fairly ordinary questions so far. Pause for a moment to think about the mathematics involved. The first image in the equivalent fractions question looks like something about patterns in the times tables, so this gives a place to start. This pattern links equivalent fractions to multiplication and division, which leads to number patterns, sequences, mappings and algebra (the 4-times table is another version of $n \rightarrow 4n$). Multiplication tables also lead to multiples, factors and common factors. Lots of mathematics is already emerging. Fortunately such connections are often explicit within official documents. Within the same section of the NNS plan is work on the number operations, which offers further advice for the teacher 'consolidating understanding of the operations of multiplication and division' (draft section 2, p. 18). How, then, to include some of this work as well?

The well-known multiplication grid offers an opportunity for looking at patterns related to division and factors as well as the more usual multiplication facts. Linking its use explicitly to equivalent fractions may enhance the understanding of the links with multiplication and division even further, especially if the table has more than the usual 10–12 rows or columns. For example, the pattern in the shaded section of the grid in Figure 10.1 gives pupils images of the fractions equivalent to $\frac{4}{5}$ in a different way.

✕	1	2	3	4	5	6	7	8	9	10	11	12	13	14	15
1	1	2	3	4	5	6	7	8	9	10	11	12	13	14	15
2	2	4	6	8	10	12	14	16	18	20	22	24	26	28	30
3	3	6	9	12	15	18	21	24	27	30	33	36	39	42	45
4	4	8	12	16	20	24	28	32	36	40	44	48	52	56	60
5	5	10	15	20	25	30	35	40	45	50	55	60	65	70	75
6	6	12	18	24	30	36	42	48	54	60					
7	7	14	21	28	35	42	49	56	6^						
8	8	16	24	32											
9	9	18	27												

Figure 10.1 Part of a multiplication grid

A stronger link to common factors can be made explicit. Finding 21 and 49 in the same column and then moving to the left along the row shows that $\frac{21}{49}$ is equivalent to $\frac{3}{7}$. If you move up the column, the column header gives the common factor. Fractions and equivalent fractions can be strongly linked to multiplication and division: i.e. $6 \div 9 = \frac{6}{9} = \frac{2}{3}$. The idea can be practised in various activities away from the grid by asking patterns of questions:

> Which multiplication table do 14 and 49 have in common?
> What common factor do 14 and 49 have?
> What is $\frac{14}{49}$ in its simplest form

Some fractions may need more than one step. For example, in simplifying $\frac{24}{120}$ we see that both numbers are in the 12-times table, and using a factor of 12 gives the fraction $\frac{2}{10}$, needing a factor of 2 to give $\frac{1}{5}$; the highest common factor is $2 \times 12 = 24$.

Finding $\frac{3}{7}$ of 56 can also be demonstrated using the grid. Find 56 in the '7' row, and move up to the '3' row, which gives you 24. This can make the links to multiplication and division for this process more explicit.

These links may be obvious to the experienced teacher, but by looking for links in the scheme when planning it is easier to create tasks which make the connections within mathematics more explicit. A splurge connecting all this mathematics might look like Figure 10.2.

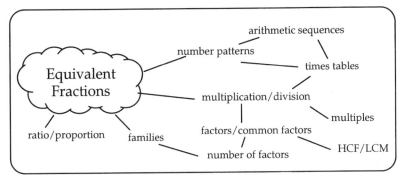

Figure 10.2 A splurge diagram for equivalent fractions

Here are a few tasks which use the multiplication grid and link some of the areas in the splurge diagram. You will need to use the idea on many occasions in order to reinforce the connections. It is of little use to ask pupils to change one fraction. The task is too easy using the grid and is unlikely to be remembered. Pupils need to look at families of fractions in order to begin to see the relationships.

The first task looks at families of fractions, the '24ths'. By doing the whole family, the idea of factors becomes a more important aspect of simplifying fractions.

> Find as many different proper fractions with 24 as the denominator, and use the multiplication grid to write them in their lowest terms. What factors are used? What are the factors of 24? Try 16 (36, 42, 60, and so on) as the denominator.

This can be a good activity to do with a fractions calculator if, on another occasion, you want to offer a very different image. Entering $\frac{1}{24}$ and using the constant function does not give the expected pattern of $\frac{1}{24} = \frac{2}{24} = \frac{3}{24} =$ but $\frac{1}{24} = \frac{1}{12} = \frac{1}{8} = \dots$ This gives an 'ooh' factor, but it does not offer links in the way that the multiplication grid does.

Finding 'fractions of' also needs to be practised in an environment which works on the links.

> Find $\frac{2}{5}$ of 45 (75, 60, 115, 120, 35, 20, 100) using the multiplication grid. How could you find $\frac{2}{5}$ of 450 (4500, 4.5)? How can you find $\frac{2}{5}$ of 240 (360)? What can you say about $\frac{2}{5}$ of 22?

The repetition allows help to be given while there is still more of the same for pupils to do. More importantly it provides clues to the mathematics of the multiples of 5 and 2. Having worked on this task, pupils could make up their own equations, which would allow you to assess their understanding of these aspects.

You might wish to connect fractions, ratio and multiplication:

Using the multiplication grid, which numbers is it easy to find $\frac{3}{7}$ of? Why? Find the missing numbers in these ratios: 9:21 and 27:63. Find some other ratio pairs. What have these ratio pairs in common with the family of fractions equivalent to $\frac{3}{7}$?

These questions are similar to those at the beginning of this section, the difference being that they provide more of the same type of practice (you have several goes before too many numbers change) and the multiplication grid offers an environment to stress the connection with multiplication and factors.

Connecting within section 3

Section 3, in Table 10.1, contains properties of shapes and coordinates. Elsewhere in this book we have combined these two topics, but we will offer another example here, remembering that once you know how to plot a coordinate, you know the definition for plotting a point, and there is not a huge amount more to know. Properties of shape, on the other hand, is quite a large area of mathematics, including congruence, symmetry and angle as well as particular properties of shapes such as the use of mid-points in the following question. The diagram in Figure 10.3 is given in the NNS (draft section 2, p. 56), where mid-points on a square are joined to find a new square. The question uses one of the learner aspects discussed in Chapter 8.

'Imagine joining adjacent mid-points of a square. Describe the new shape formed.'

Properties of shape/coordinates

Using ideas of changing and adding givens from Chapter 4, this question might be adapted to practising coordinates by defining the vertices by coordinate pairs. The role of the coordinates is strengthened by looking at any patterns which help to identify 'middleness'.

Draw a square whose vertices are at the points (3, 2), (11, 2), (11, 10) and (3, 10). Find the mid-points of each side (write down their coordinates), and join these points. What is the new shape? Repeat the process in the new shape. What happens? Why? What do you notice about the coordinates?
If the vertices of the first square had the coordinates (7, 9), (23, 9), (23, 25) and (7, 25), what would be the coordinates of the second and third shapes? Why?

The task still focuses on the property of the shape but also allows exploration of the connection of mid-points of line segments and their relation to the coordinates of the end points. Immediately, the idea of changing one of the givens in this task occurs: 'what-if-not' a square, but any other quadrilateral? Does anything special happen?

Properties of shape: congruence/symmetry/angle
The examples in NNS (draft section 2, p. 65) offer questions where the properties of shape are linked to coordinate questions:

> The points (–5, –3), (–1, 2) and (3, –1) are the vertices of a triangle. Identify where the vertices lie after:
> - translation of 3 units to the right;
> - reflection in the x-axis;
> - rotation of 180° about the origin.

If we think about the mathematics, each of these transformations preserves shape: each image is congruent to the object. A more open question which links coordinates and congruent triangles is:

> Draw the triangle which has the vertices (–2, 5), (–3, 10) and (1, 7). Draw some triangles congruent to this where one of the vertices is at (–2, –7).

This may seem too complicated, but you can help pupils with two or three examples and still leave them with work to do. Which translations work? Don't forget the rotations and reflections.

Properties of shape with Ma1
Each of the tasks below has more than one answer and gives more practice than the questions in the NNS, which are intended for more formal assessment purposes.

> If (1, 1) and (1, 7) are two of the vertices of a quadrilateral, find some examples of the coordinates of the other two vertices if the quadrilateral has:
> - at least two sides equal in length;
> - at least two sides equal in length and a reflex angle;
> - diagonals which are equal in length;
> - one line of symmetry.

You can challenge some pupils to generalise their findings while others stay with the more obvious aspects of the task.

Linking across sections

Properties of shape with fractions
The work on coordinates can be linked to the properties of shape, and shape also appears in the work on fractions, suggesting tasks which ask pupils to use all of these ideas:

> Plot the points (5, 1), (9, 5), (5, 9), (1, 5) and (5, 1) and join them up in order. Name the shape you have drawn. Join the points (5, 1), (5, 3) and (3, 3). What shapes can you see in the diagram. Shade the smallest shape. What fraction is this shape of the whole shape?

This is a fairly closed task, but you could ask about the fractions of all the other shapes. To provide more challenge the pupils could create their own designs to be checked by others.

> Draw different parallelograms which have two of their vertices at (1, 2) and (11, 8). Try to shade a third of the diagram. For which sets of points is this easier?

Properties of shape with equations
Equations and formulas may seem to be separate but these could be practised in the context of shape.

> Draw some examples of rectangles whose length is s and whose width is t where $s = t + 3$. Find the area and perimeter of each rectangle.

> For different values of x, draw some examples of rectangles whose length is $x + 2$ and whose width is x. Find the area and perimeter of each rectangle. Explain your findings.

Coordinates/shape/symmetry

> A rhombus (with vertices at whole number coordinates) has one line of symmetry which joins the vertices (1, 3) and (1, 7). Draw some examples. Find the area of each rhombus drawn. Where are the vertices of the rhombus if the area is 4cm², 8cm², 12cm², etc.? Why?

The end of the question may seem too complex, but this could just be there to challenge your brightest pupils while others are working on the main part of the task.

> Draw a trapezium with $y = 3$ as a line of symmetry. Which coordinates are related to others? How?

Coordinates and equations
Equations and coordinates are strongly linked by the equations of lines, but you may not want to formalise the equations of lines at this early stage. They could, however, be used as contexts for practising and understanding the role of substituting and variables.

> Plot some coordinates (x, y) where $x + y = 7$. What do you notice?

The equation is in this form because many children understand the idea of two numbers adding to 7, before you formalise your work on equations.

Properties of shape with probability
Probability lies in a section of its own but the emphasis in the key objectives on the value of probability being between 0 and 1 gives a well-used link to fractions, decimals and percentages. The connection could be stressed by expecting answers to probability questions to be given in the three different forms (fraction, decimal and percentage). Using three forms of number line (Figure 10.3) can also be valuable.

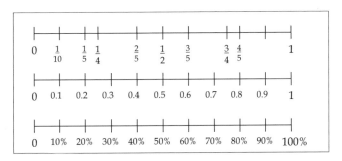

Figure 10.3 Fractions, decimals and percentage lines

How might you connect probability and shape? Probability can be practised using materials involving shape properties. Shape cards are easily made and can be used for work on properties, but for probability pupils could be asked to choose a subset of the cards – naming the set – and then answer questions:

> What is the probability of picking a card, at random, so that it shows a square?
> What is the probability of picking a card, at random, so that it shows a shape with one line of symmetry?
> What is the probability of picking a card, at random, so that it shows a shape with at least one right angle?

Once you are practised at combining topics you may want to extend the challenge to include more topics. Here are some more suggestions.

Area/perimeter/sequences/using a calculator/decimals

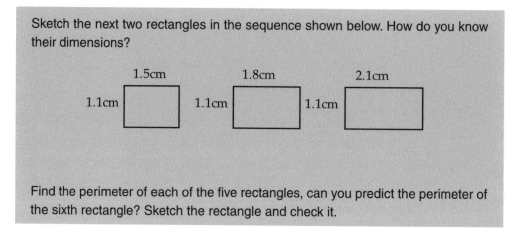

Sketch the next two rectangles in the sequence shown below. How do you know their dimensions?

Find the perimeter of each of the five rectangles, can you predict the perimeter of the sixth rectangle? Sketch the rectangle and check it.

Area/perimeter/calculator use/decimal places/metric units
Conversion from centimetres to metres or vice versa is rarely given any real context, so by choosing to calculate area/perimeter on larger figures this aspect can be explored.

Find the area and perimeter of a rectangle measuring 1.76m × 1.25m.

Pupils often lack any referents for area so a useful resource would be a metre square of material to fold to demonstrate half and a quarter of a metre square. It would be valuable to work with a full size diagram (Figure 10.4) in the hall or out on the playground.

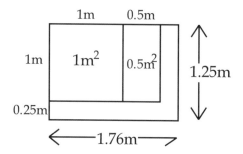

Figure 10.4 Dividing a rectangle

By considering the area in the question as 176cm × 125cm, the comparison can be related to the area of the rectangles to enable discussion of conversion: how many square centimetres are equivalent to a square metre?

Scale drawing would offer another dimension to the task and allow stronger comparisons. The task could be adapted to a context which allows another way of thinking of the units:

> What if area is to be covered by carpet tiles, each measuring a quarter of a metre squared?

If you have answers in both square centimetres and square metres, these can be compared using significant figures or decimal places.

Volume/metric units/calculator use/approximation
This task expects you to use resources: models of open cuboids and some containers – pop bottles and cans – some of which are labelled, and some not.

> Given a litre cube (10cm × 10cm × 10cm) – find the volume of different shapes in cubic centimetres and litres, initially by deciding whether they will hold more or less than a litre and then calculating their volume.

Pupils are not asked to estimate, but, in fact, they are estimating relative to a litre. The connection within the units is stressed in the next task.

> How many cubic centimetres fit into a cubic metre? How many litres fit into a cubic metre? How many multilink cubes will fill into a cubic metre? (The multilink cube measures approximately 2cm × 2cm × 2cm.)

Both tasks offer referents for volume/capacity as well as the conversion of metric units. By connecting the two tasks the connection between cubic centimetres, cubic metres and litres can be made more explicit.

Area/perimeter/imperial–metric conversion/calculator use

> Draw a square of side 5 inches, using 2mm graph paper, and a ruler with inches. Draw a square of side 5cm. Find the perimeter of both squares in centimetres. What is the ratio of the perimeters? Why? Find the areas of both squares in square centimetres. What is the ratio of the areas? Repeat for squares or rectangles of different sizes.

Coordinates/area of compound shapes/percentages

> On 1cm graph paper with axes $0 \leq x \leq 10$ and $0 \leq y \leq 10$, plot the points (2, 2), (8,
> 2), (8, 4), (4, 4), (4, 8), (2, 8) and (2,2) and join them up in order. Find the area of
> the shape. Sketch and label the lengths of sides of two possible rectangles into
> which the shape could be divided. Find their areas and perimeters. Are the sums
> of their areas and perimeters the same as the area and perimeter of the
> hexagon? Why? What percentage of the area of the 10cm × 10cm square is the
> area of the hexagon?

The diagram will look like Figure 10.7. A standard question has been adapted to
percentages by the addition of the 10cm × 10cm square. More complex
approaches to percentages can be gained by changing the dimensions of the two
parts of the diagram.

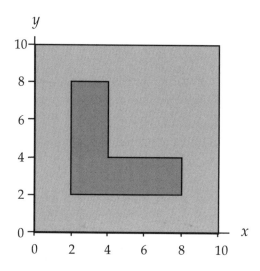

Figure 10.5 A hexagon

Your pupils could do the designing themselves. The practice on coordinates is
likely to be lost unless each pupil has to write the instructions for someone else to
draw the same diagram. This can be a very useful extension; the pupils are also
doing some of your marking.

> Draw a hexagon with area 16% of the space enclosed by the square axes. Justify
> your answer. Draw other hexagons with area 16% of the square space. Which has
> the largest perimeter? If the axes are $0 \leq x \leq 5$ and $0 \leq y \leq 5$, draw a hexagon with
> area 64% of the space enclosed by the square axes.

Mappings/area/perimeter

Draw some rectangles which are 1cm longer than they are wide. Draw up a mapping table for:

width   → length
width   → perimeter
length → perimeter
width   → area
length → area

Capacity/volume/statistics/decimals

Estimate the capacity of five cuboids to the nearest tenth of a litre. From the class data plot a frequency diagram and calculate the mean, mode and median. Calculate the capacity of the cuboids, and draw a diagram to compare the real and estimated capacities.

Does practice make us better? Repeat the experiment with five new models. Compare the results.

And finally

Syllabus lists can appear daunting. They can seem to split the maths curriculum into lots of small bits. Each small bit can look like a topic for individual lessons, making too many lessons for the time available. The only way to manage this apparently over-large content is to connect the curriculum. Connecting the curriculum is recommended by the National Curriculum (DfEE 1999).

> At key stages 3 and 4, teaching should ensure that appropriate connections are made between the sections on number and algebra; shape, space and measures; and handling data.
> (DfEE 1999: 6)

If we design activities that connect the mathematical content in as many different ways as possible, you can make the syllabus more manageable. You can also offer opportunities for more practice and work on the learning of mathematics more efficiently.

References

Department for Education and Employment (DfEE) (1999) *Mathematics: The National Curriculum for England.* London: The Stationery Office.
Department for Education and Employment (DfEE) (2000) *The National Numeracy Strategy – Framework for Teaching Mathematics: Year 7.* Draft 3/00. London: DfEE. www.standards.dfee.gov.uk/numeracy/NNSframework (accessed 23 November 2000).

CHAPTER 11

And so to choose

This chapter summarises some of the infinite consequences of teacher choices and shows how to apply a concertina strategy to any task. Oh, and as for the mathematics, as E. M. Forster would have said, 'Only connect!'

No task is only a starter or a main meal or a pudding. Nobody always wants a three-course meal – just a pudding can be sublime! From the evidence of the previous chapters any task can be altered, amended, extended or contracted to suit your purpose. We hear a lot about the three-part lesson but sometimes, depending on the weather, the furniture in the room, the time of day, day of the week and the month of the year, the curriculum subject taught in the preceding lesson, and so on, we might want something different: the choice is yours. You might decide to challenge and motivate differently – with a two-part lesson or a seven-part lesson or a one-part lesson. The permutations and combinations of a lesson plan are infinitely changeable but fortunately tangible. You can never be certain what another human being might learn in your classroom but you must be certain about the opportunity for mathematics to be done that day and you must be certain how this mathematics connects to the syllabus, to the NNS and to the National Curriculum. Remember, the pupils are with you for at least five years. It is alright to have long-term goals as well as short-term ones.

In previous chapters we have offered you ways to change existing tasks and to analyse the mathematics to help you in your choice of suitable tasks. The final choice we offer is that of time. Different lengths of time allow an activity to suit different purposes. We will start with short activities, using ideas stolen from elsewhere, and see how these might be created. Then we will extend some of these to larger tasks. We realise that one of the major agents for the change to longer and more challenging tasks is Ma1, discussed in earlier chapters. Here we tweak some activities, some more than others, with a time factor to suit practice, revision, exploration, etc.

Short activities: beginnings and ends

Given the emphasis the NNS places on short aural activities and mental methods it is worth starting with some of these ideas. We have looked at some of the ideas that are in the Framework and in related texts and schemes. Then we analysed these in terms of the mathematics, the resources and the type of actions, separating the mathematics out of the activity. The results are grouped in three columns in Table 11.1.

Table 11.1 Pick and mix

Mathematics	Resources	Actions
Fractions, decimals and percentages	(D) Diagrams	(C) Chanting
	(F) Flash cards	(E) Explaining their own methods
Conversion to and from fractions, decimals and percentages	(G) Games	
	(N) Number cards	(M) Moving
Rounding		(P) Playing games
	(T) Technology: a spreadsheet, calculators, etc.	
Inverse operations		(Q) Question and answer
Variables		(W) Writing

We have done this to show how to maximise your choices as a teacher. Add to the columns by stealing as many ideas as you can from other people. Adapt them by using different resources and different mathematics. Versatility is needed here so to practise some mathematics perm any one item from each of the three columns to create a short activity.

Here are some suggestions using some of the mathematics content from column 1 and then the types of resources and actions from columns 2 and 3. All of the first few activities practise equivalences of fractions, decimals and percentages. These activities could be used for 'reminders' or 'summaries', depending on what happened in the previous day's lesson, what is about to happen in that day's lesson or what actually happened in the lesson. It is your choice, but the activity must have significance for the learner. The details of the first few are given but, no doubt, if you have got this far in the book, you could probably generate your own – and better. The only other thing to say about these activities is that they are only 'quick' if the pupils have some sense of how to answer the questions. (There would be no point in doing these if the pupils cannot access the knowledge. Apologies if this is obvious.)

The first activity practises the mathematics in a snap game. Cards are created with different fractions and decimals. You also decide the level of difficulty and challenge with the set of numbers that you choose to use, depending on which class you are working with.

 Play fractions/decimals snap.

You could extend the game and add in percentages. The second game is also a card game but in the form of loop dominoes (see Chapter 6).

 Use loop dominoes for fraction/decimal/percentage equivalence.

Next you might imagine a large set of snap cards which you could use to hold up for all the class to see.

 Hold up flash cards showing fractions, pupils chant the corresponding decimal.

Or, indeed, you could set this up on a spreadsheet if you have a computer and large screen in your classroom.

 Use the random number function on a spreadsheet to generate a decimal. Pupils chant the corresponding fraction or percentage.

Next, supposing that the lesson needs to start peacefully (so no chanting). We move on to some written work.

Write down three ways to calculate 17.5% of $50.

Or maybe they all need waking up with an activity which requires them to move about!

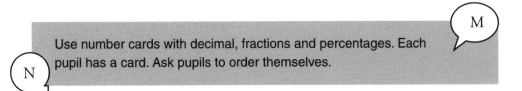

No doubt by now you will be able to alter each of the above to get many new versions. Other ideas begin to fly: use loop domino cards of miles/kilometres to use a conversion graph; play similar shapes snap; hold up flash cards of shapes to chant the names or write the name to practise spelling. Hold up flash cards with numbers on to practise some arithmetic, change some of the numbers to letters, and, hey presto, they are practising creating expressions and dealing with variables. The variation is almost infinite. But we have found that pupils like repetition (think how many games of noughts and crosses you played as a child) so it is comforting for them (and probably for you, as there is need for less explanation) to repeat activities time and again.

The polypede (our name for a circle with lines radiating from it) has infinite variation. Imagine the polypede in Figure 11.1 on the board with some numbers around the outside.

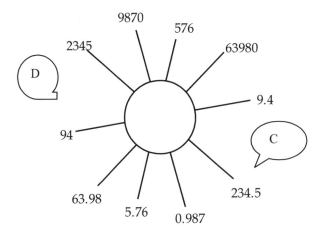

Figure 11.1 Number polypede

The instruction in the middle might be to 'round to the nearest ten', 'multiply by 10^2', or 'divide by 10^n'. Any of these could happen as a chanting session to check a facility with powers of ten or rounding. Or pupils could copy the diagram and write the answers quietly, as a warm-up or cool-down or a rehearsal for homework.

Suppose you want the pupils to practise some algebra. An opening (or closing) chanting session might have a number in the middle and expressions around the outside and could be used for a lesson on algebraic substitution with manageable numbers and expressions (but what does manageable look like?) (Figure 11.2).

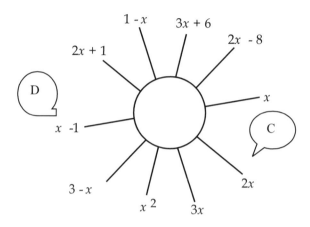

Figure 11.2 Algebra polypede

The pupils could write their responses as before, but chanting has an advantage in the earlier practice stages because you can develop a routine to encourage techniques. If you put 7 in the middle, and point to x, the pupils chant "7". Point to $2x$ next, then to $2x+1$, then back to x, and then to $2x$, then to $2x - 8$ then to $2x - 8$, developing a routine which reminds the pupils of the order of substitution.

From little to large

The art of good teaching is choosing good activities for the learner and knowing where the learners are in terms of their mathematics. As we said above short activities are not short if the pupils cannot do the mathematics. The next challenge is to take one of the short activities, imagine a class that could not do it and recreate it as a more extended task.

Let's take the first activity from the previous section.

G   Play fractions/decimals snap.   P

For children who cannot recall the equivalences, this will be a slow game. You may need to let the pupils sort the cards before they play snap. The class could be allowed to play the game for longer, if you feel they need the practice. You could even have a tournament. The same activity can be used for a different length of time depending on how you choose to design your lesson.

Take the second idea from above.

G   Use loop dominoes for fraction/decimal/percentage equivalence.   P

First, to get the contrast, imagine a Year 9 class that needs to practise recognising the common equivalences (½, 0.5, 50%; ¾, 0.75, 75%; etc.). This activity is a short activity, taking only five minutes if the pupils are awake! Now imagine a Year 7 group who are meeting these equivalences for the first time or who are working on changing between the different number sets. Armed with a calculator and a set of challenging loop cards this activity could last for the lesson while they practise the techniques of changing from one to another. They could work collaboratively on this task. It is an understanding of the possibilities in the mathematics and progression in the mathematics across the year groups which changes the task from starter to main course. Going back to the bright Year 9 class, this activity becomes a bit longer if you create a domino set which has repetition of the numbers and the Year 9 pupils are asked to find the number of different subsets that make a closed loop and offer justification for their solution.

The polypede in Figure 11.1 could become a longer activity if given as a sheet to pairs of pupils who are asked to find 'the relationship between the numbers in the opposite diagonals' with the aim being to work towards standard form. A longer lesson with the algebraic polypede (Figure 11.2) might be for a number chosen by the pupils to be put in the middle for them to find the values of the expressions around the spokes; linear, quadratic or cubic depending on the group. The challenge might be to find a number (or two or three) for the middle that gives two (or three or more) of the expressions the same value. And so we have a lesson on simultaneous equations with a variety of data to explore 'why this happens' and a move to justification and proof. Alternatively, another longer lesson might be to select two of the expressions to find the coordinates of the point(s) of intersection; in fact, to select all possible pairs in turn might create work for a week.

From large to little

It is also possible to contract some of your bigger tasks or use the same tasks with different age and attainment ranges. Remember the bar chart from Chapter 4? Version 6 gave the frequency and mean and asked for the missing bars to be put on to the chart. The first choice in changing the task was to remove some of the givens. The second choice is to set it up as a short activity.

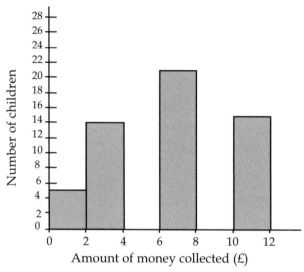

Figure 11.3 Bar chart showing the amount of money collected by children on a sponsored walk

This is a meaty task if all these mathematical ideas have only recently been met. But imagine setting this up on a spreadsheet and presenting it on a large screen at the beginning of a lesson with Year 11 pupils who are revising for GCSE. The chart could go up with the two missing bars and the pupils could be asked the possible sizes of bars for total frequencies. You might add in the calculation of the mean if they are quick to respond, given that four of the products always remain the same.

The activity given about triangles in Chapter 3 was changed into a lengthy task for a class just beginning to practise angle sum of a triangle, as well as some algebra, by changing one of the givens. Once your pupils can do this level of substitution it is no longer a long task. To a higher attaining class this activity becomes a warm-up. It may be just a revision of angles in a triangle and substitution but it could be prelude to creating and solving the equations $b = 3a$ and $c = 180 - 4a$, and plotting the relationship between b and c as a varies (Figure 11.4).

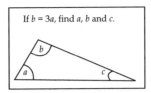

Figure 11.4 Angles in a triangle

Little and large

If we take the task of finding the area of the hexagon in Chapter 5, the original question takes as long as the pupils need, unless they can get the teacher to do it for them. Version 2 (Figure 11.5) takes not much longer, even though there is an extra decision, so it could be a short task. If the pupils know how to do the task, it can become a quick question which acts as revision.

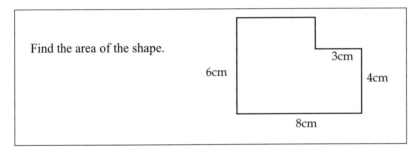

Figure 11.5 Area of a compound shape, version 2

Pupils could work on the more open version (Figure 11.6) for a long time before generalisation occurs. Then you might want to spend time on proof.

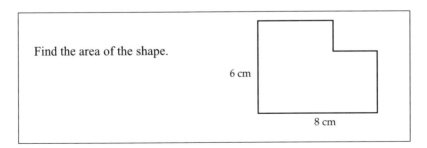

Figure 11.6 Area of a compound shape, version 3

But the open question could be used as a short task, offering the pupils the choice of numbers to use. Or you could tweak the task by giving the area, say 40cm^2, and asking for the missing dimensions. If you had Omnigraph for Windows on a large screen in your teaching room, it is easy for pupils to suggest coordinates and let the software find the area; a different form of revision. A time limit changes the level of pressure. You can change the focus of the task by changing the timing.

The coffee bean task in Chapter 9 could be used as a short activity to practise reading a table and calculating the price for a mix of two types of coffee. It could become a regular five-minute task.

Coffee made from a mix of two, three or four types of beans, Javan, Columbian, Kenyan and Continental roast, is sold. The coffee is delivered from its store barrel in 25g scoops. If I buy 500g of coffee, how much of each type of bean is this?

How much will the coffee cost?

Beans	Price per 100g
House roast	£0.83
Continental roast	£1.04
Columbia	£0.92
Java	£1.14
Kenya	£1.13

Can I spend exactly £4, if I can choose any mix of coffee?

If you were to try to spend exactly £4, the task, even using a spreadsheet (Figure 11.7) could be longer as alternative solutions are found. But again it could be a short task using a large screen attached to your computer, allowing the class to test ideas collectively.

	A	B Price per 100g	C Price per 25g	D Number of scoops	E Price	F
1	Beans					
2	House Roast	£0.83	£0.21	12	£2.49	
3	Continental Roast	£1.04	£0.26	0	£0.00	
4	Columbia	£0.92	£0.23	0	£0.00	
5	Java	£1.14	£0.29	8	£2.28	
6	Kenya	£1.13	£0.28	0	£0.00	
7			Total grammes	500	£4.77	

Figure 11.7 Spreadsheet for coffee beans

The longer pupils spend on a task, the more likely they are to be working on the processes of Ma1. But even short tasks can be accompanied by the expectation of explanation and justification, as in explaining why the area of a hexagon in Figure 11.6 could be 40cm^2.

Summary

This book has offered you a number of strategies for adapting and extending tasks. To add to all the other possible changes presented, this chapter has considered how the emphasis of tasks changes according to the time allowed. Why do we change tasks? Sometimes pupils have found a particular question difficult, so we want to practise the same mathematics in a different way. Sometimes we want to offer a similar question for homework. Sometimes pupils need more practice at certain aspects, so we offer more of the same, but with a different mathematical purpose. And for our brightest we want to be able to stretch their thinking, to get them to explore the breadth of the mathematics. Extending pupil choices within a task demands a higher level of responsibility from the learner and integrates the processes of Ma1.

The splurge diagram in Figure 11.8 summarises the different ways we have changed tasks in this book. Throughout the book there is the constant reminder to analyse the mathematics; for example, resources, especially technology, can significantly change the way that your pupils access the mathematics. These changes may happen in your planning, or they may happen in the moment as you respond to your pupils' mathematical needs. There are many, many choices you can make. Each choice has its own implications for the learning of mathematics.

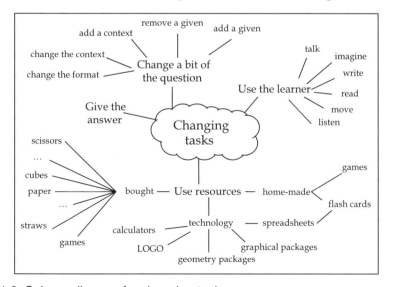

Figure 11.8 Splurge diagram for changing tasks

References

Bond, M. (1971) *Paddington at Large*. London: Collins.

Brown, S. I. and Walter, M. I. (1990) *The Art of Problem Posing*, 2nd edn. London: Lawrence Erlbaum Associates.

Department for Education and Employment (DfEE) (1999) *Mathematics: The National Curriculum for England*. London: The Stationery Office.

Department for Education and Employment (DfEE) (2000) *The National Numeracy Strategy – Framework for Teaching Mathematics: Year 7*. Draft 3/00. London: DfEE. www.standards.dfee.gov.uk/numeracy/NNSframework (accessed November 2000).

Fynn (1974) *Mister God, This is Anna*. London: William Collins.

Graham, A. (1991) 'Where is the "P" in statistics?', in Pimm, D. and Love, E. (eds) *Teaching and Learning School Mathematics*. London: Hodder & Stoughton.

Hewitt, D. (1999) 'Arbitrary and necessary, part 1: a way of viewing the mathematics curriculum', *For the Learning of Mathematics* **19**(3), 2–9.

Mason, J. (1991) Inaugural address as Professor of Mathematics Education. Milton Keynes: Open University.

Perks, P. and Prestage, S. (1992) 'Making choices (3): choices, constraints and control', *Mathematics in Schools* **21**(5), 44–5.

Perks, P. and Prestage, S. (1994) 'Planning for learning', in Jaworski, B. and Watson, A. (eds) *Mentoring in Mathematics Teaching*. London: Falmer.

School Mathematics Project (1985) *SMP 11–16 Book B2*. Cambridge: Cambridge University Press.

Software

A useful link to software is mathsnet: www.anglia.co.uk/education/mathsnet

There are other geometry packages but we are most familiar with Cabri-Géomètre www.cabri.imag.fr/index-e.html and The Geometer's Sketchpad, www.keypress.com

The LOGO used in this book is MSWLogo, available from www.softronix.com

Locate is a game from MicroSMILE for Windows, 'Pack 5: Coordinates', www.smile mathematics.co.uk

Omnigraph for Windows is available from SPA, www.spasoft.co.uk

Many spreadsheet programs are available. Our examples have been constructed with Microsoft Excel. The calculator particularly mentioned is Texas Instruments TI92, www.ti.com/calc/docs/calchome.htm

N.B. Each of these sites were accessed by the authors in October/November 2000.

Index

130 Great Irish Ballads

Introduction to 1st Edition - 1997

This book took me two years to produce. The idea sprang out of my love of music - traditional Irish music and ballads in particular.

Each of these songs I have sung at one time or another in the past. Usually in pubs. A sure sign of a mis-spent youth! But what a way to mis-spend it! The songs are ever present all around me - on faded bits of paper, in my head, captured in the soundbox of my guitar and banjo.

So I decided to compile and arrange them into one book - my version of the songs, the lyrics, the guitar chords - and here it is!

Although all of these songs are 'great Irish ballads' it's fair to say that a small number of them originated in other lands in the dim and distant past. But they have been sung by so many Irish balladeers on so many occasions up and down the length and breadth of Ireland that they have been adopted as full-blooded Irish ballads. They have found their natural home!

So enjoy these songs! Sing them! Change the words or music or timing if you feel something else works better for you! After all, that's what ballads are all about!

A Big Thank You

There are many people who encouraged and helped me with this book. I would like to thank Trish Ryan, Sharon Murphy and Dec "I'll get this C diminished to work if it kills me" O'Brien for all of the practical help they gave me.

But in particular I would like to give special thanks to Karen O'Mahony from the Mechanical Copyright Protection Society for the countless hours she spent trying to unravel the maze of copyright control on these songs. Without her help I doubt if this book would exist today.

The CD

If you are not familiar with the particular melody of a song and can't read music the accompanying CD will provide you with the tune. I have coupled some songs together on the CD (marked 'a' and 'b' on the particular tracks) because I think that they go well together – either through the melody, tempo or theme.

The Chorus

If a song has a chorus it is printed in bold italics *like this*. Some songs start with a chorus and therefore it will be in the main body of the score. Others have the chorus after the first verse.

Choruses are great things – they are a law unto themselves. You can add more in (and this normally depends on the number of verses the singer knows!) or take them out if you want to shorten the song. So do your own thing! Do it your way!

But above all, enjoy these songs! They are crying out to be sung!

Robert Gogan

Preface to 2nd Edition

Much beer drinking, story telling, ballad singing and general shenanigans has taken place since the publication of the first edition of this book!

And up to the time I compiled the original book I had been quite content to merely sing and enjoy these great Irish ballads.

But since then my curiosity about these ballads has been aroused, fuelled to a great extent by the reaction of the readers of the first edition. I have received many queries about the ballads together with different versions from all over the world. So I began to develop a desire to know more about the ballads – what's the story behind them, who wrote them, when and where did they first appear?

So the quest started! Many reference books have been thumbed, libraries visited and websites trawled and the results are here in the second edition of my ballad book.

Is the quest over? Not, I'm afraid, by a long shot! I have discovered that several of these fine and well crafted ballads simply exist in the here-and-now, as if moulded from the very clay beneath our feet. I can find little or no information about who wrote them, the circumstances under which they were written, the characters portrayed in them or their origin. This has been a source of great frustration to me.

As a contrast I have collected reams and reams of information about several of the ballads and I have abridged the data in some cases to prevent 'information overload'.

I am also most grateful to my good friend, historian and author Éamonn MacThomáis, now sadly no longer with us. Over long conversations as we drove around Dublin Éamonn would explain in great detail the local backgrounds to some of the Dublin ballads and I am delighted to be able to pass on his knowledge and wisdom in this book.

I am also indebted to the following publications and websites for facts, information and references and for pointing me in the right direction:

"The Petrie Collection of Ancient Music of Ireland" edited by David Cooper. Cork University Press
"The Irish Music Manuscripts of Edward Bunting (1773 - 1843). An Introduction and Catalogue" edited by Colette Moloney. Irish Traditional Music Archive.
"Folksongs of Britain and Ireland" edited by Peter Kennedy. Cassell
"The Complete Guide to Celtic Music" by June Skinner Sawyers. Aurum Press
"The Age of Revolution in the Irish Song Tradition 1776 - 1815" edited by Terry Moylan. Lilliput Press
"Songs of Irish Rebellion" by Georges-Denis Zimmerman. Allen Figgis
"Irish Ballads" edited by Fleur Robertson. Gill & MacMillan
"The Poolbeg Book of Irish Ballads" by Sean McMahon. Poolbeg Press
"The '98 Reader" edited by Padraic O'Farrell. Lilliput Press
"The Oxford Companion to Irish History" edited by S.J. Connolly. Oxford University Press
"The Year of Liberty" by Thomas Pakenham. Abacus
"The Easter Rebellion" by Max Caulfield. Gill & MacMillan
"Bird Life in Ireland" by Don Conroy & Jim Wilson. The O'Brien Press
"AA Illustrated Road Book of Ireland" Automobile Association

www.contemplator.com/folk
www.mudcat.org
www.standingstones.com
www.kued.org/joehill
www.geocities.com/shantysong

Robert Gogan